Samuel French Acting Edition

D

MW01094819

by Colman Domingo

FOR PRODUCTION ENQUIRIES

UNITED STATES AND CANADA
Info@SamuelFrench.com
1-866-598-8449

UNITED KINGDOM AND EUROPE
Plays@SamuelFrench.co.uk
020-7255-4302

Each title is subject to availability from Samuel French, depending upon country of performance. Please be aware that *DOT* may not be licensed by Samuel French in your territory. Professional and amateur producers should contact the nearest Samuel French office or licensing partner to verify availability.

MUSIC USE NOTE

IMPORTANT BILLING AND CREDIT REQUIREMENTS

DOT was first produced by the Actors Theatre of Louisville (Les Waters, Artistic Director) in Kentucky as part of their 2015 Humana Festival. The performance was directed by Meredith McDonough, with sets by Dane Laffrey, costumes by Connie Furr Soloman, lights by Mark Barton, sound by Christian Frederickson, casting by Kelly Gillespie, dramaturgy by Kimberly Colburn, and assistant direction by Rachel Dart. The Production Stage Manager was Stephen Horton and the Assistant Stage Manager was Jason Pacella. The cast was as follows:

DOTTY	Marjorie Johnson
SHELLY	Sharon Washington
JACKIE	Megan Byrne
DONNIE	Kevin R . Free
ADAM	Sean Dugan
AVERIE	Adrienne C. Moore
FIDEL	Vichet Chum

DOT received its New York premiere at the Vineyard Theater (Douglas Aibel and Sarah Stern, Artistic Directors; Jennifer Garvey-Blackwell, Executive Director) on February 23, 2016. The performance was directed by Susan Stroman, with associate direciton by Eric Santagata, sets by Allen Moyer, costumes by Kara Harmon, lights by Ben Stanton, sound by Tom Morse, and hair and makeup by Dave Bova. The Production Stage Manager was Roy Harris, and the production supervisor was Roy Harris. The cast was as follows:

DOTTY	Marjorie Johnson
SHELLY	Sharon Washington
JACKIE	Finnerty Steeves
DONNIE	Stephen Conrad Moore
ADAM	Colin Hanlon
AVERIE	Libya V. Pugh
FIDEL	Michael Rosen

CHARACTERS

DOTTY – African American. Sixty-five years old.

SHELLY – African American. Forty-five years old.

JACKIE – Caucasian. Forty years old.

DONNIE – African American. Forty years old.

ADAM – Caucasian/Latin/Arab. Forty years old.

AVERIE – African American. Thirty-five years old.

FIDEL – Kazakh. Mid-to-late twenties.

SETTING

Philadelphia, Pennsylvania

TIME

Two days before Christmas and Christmas Eve

AUTHOR'S NOTES

// Denotes overlaps. Silences are to be used as a silent opportunity. If you run into a few of them, give them the weight that they deserve. Don't rush them. They are as important as rests in music. These characters speak before they think. The people that I know in West Philly have the dryest delivery. Especially about difficult subjects or even saying I love you. Try not putting anything on a line first and read it for its rhythms, and then go deeper. No one in this play is deliberately mean or callous. The stakes are just too high and there is no need to mince words. And these people are lightning-quick with shifts of tone or intention. Brace yourselves. Welcome to *Dot*.

This play is for Stacey Thomas, Lisa Thompson, Anika Noni Rose, Chuck Schultz, Lorrie Sargent, and the amazing women that live on in their memory. This is for families that are coping and finding their way. And everything I do, I do in honor of my parents, Edith and Clarence Bowles; The Domingo, Hawkins, and Bowles families; and Raul Aktanov-Domingo. Thank you Les Waters, Meredith McDonough, Sean San Jose, Susan Stroman, Jen Garvey Blackwell, Doug Aibel, Sarah Stern, Jim Nicola, Linda Chapman, Sharon Washington, and Marjorie Johnson, and every generous actor and artisan that helped me in the stages of development to realize this play called Dot.

THE NORTHERN LIGHTS

("MY FAVORITE THINGS" sung by Tony Bennett*
plays as we open on three women in a beautiful,
upscale kitchen. Very Martha Stewart meets Claire
Huxtable. **DOTTY** *is a sixty-five-year-old African*
American woman. **SHELLY** *is her forty-fiive-year-*
old daughter. **JACKIE** *is forty years old, Caucasian.*
DOTTY *is looking at a pill container with segments*
for each day of the week. **SHELLY** *is by the fridge*
with a Watermelon Vodka bottle. **JACKIE** *has just*
arrived. Everyone is a bit on edge. **DOTTY** *is*
obsessive, almost compulsive about her thoughts
this morning. She is not in a lovely mood and she
thinks lighting-quick.)

DOTTY. Today is Tuesday?

SHELLY. Yes, today is Tuesday.

DOTTY. Christmas is in two days.

SHELLY. I know Mom, I know.

DOTTY. You getting the tree today?

SHELLY. Yes, I told you ten times, I'm getting the tree today. Jackie you sure you don't want a drink?

JACKIE. It's almost ten o'clock in the morning.

SHELLY. Are you sure?

JACKIE. Yes.

SHELLY. I'm having one.

JACKIE. No, no thank you.

SHELLY. A.A. or something?

JACKIE. No, it's just –

---

* A license to produce *Dot* does not include a performance license for "My Favorite Things." Please see Music Use Note on page 3 for further information.

DOTTY. I could swear I took 'em this morning when Fidel came by!

SHELLY. Fidel came by yesterday morning.

JACKIE. Mrs. Shealy, Shelly, I can come back later.

DOTTY. *(To* **SHELLY**.*)* You sure?

SHELLY. Yes, he comes on Monday and Wednesday and sometimes Friday.

JACKIE. Fidel?

SHELLY. Yes, Fidel.

JACKIE. Who's Fidel?

SHELLY. This boy that – Give me few minutes and we can have a proper visit. In the other room.

JACKIE. I just came to borrow some linen from your mom.

SHELLY. Mom, I need you to sign that! *(She lays a folder and a pen on the table.)* You didn't sign it.

DOTTY. Don't I need a lawyer to be present or something?

SHELLY. I am a lawyer, remember?

DOTTY. Eight years of school! And you failed the Pennsylvania bar three times, I remember.

SHELLY. Sign it. She's your witness.

JACKIE. Who?

DOTTY. Three times.

SHELLY. You.

JACKIE. For what?

SHELLY. Don't worry about it, it's all legal – Mom please sign!

DOTTY. Oh, okay I will. On the dotted line, on the dotted line. *(She picks up the pen, and then she gets distracted.)* Good ole Jackie! How you doing?

JACKIE. I'm fine, Mrs. Shealy.

DOTTY. Ain't seen you in awhile.

JACKIE. It's been a while.

DOTTY. You still living in New York?

JACKIE. Yes, Mrs. Shealy.

DOTTY. You can call me Dotty now, honey, you a grown woman.

JACKIE. Yes, Mrs. Shealy, I am still living in New York. Maybe this is a bad time?

SHELLY. It's all the same.

DOTTY. Where?

JACKIE. Where what?

DOTTY. Where do you live in New York?

JACKIE. Oh! Um, Harlem.

DOTTY. Is it still dirty?

JACKIE. When is the last time you been there?

DOTTY. '83.

SHELLY. Mom, do you want eggs?

DOTTY. What time is it?

SHELLY. Ten o'clock. Mom you need to eat. Do you want eggs?

DOTTY. Yes I want eggs. I can make my own eggs.

> (*She gets up to make her eggs.* **SHELLY** *stops her and makes the eggs.*)

SHELLY. Mom, I thought we agreed that I will make breakfast and you will make dinner.

DOTTY. Is that what we agreed on?

SHELLY. Yes, that's what we agreed on.

JACKIE. I can just come back –

SHELLY. (*Sotto voce.*) Just give me a minute –

DOTTY. Just don't put cheese in it. Richard always puts cheese in my eggs.

SHELLY. Richard? Mom? Dad? SHIT!

DOTTY. Language –

SHELLY. Never mind.

DOTTY. I told you I wanted to stop all that unnecessary cussin' in this house.

SHELLY. Look who's talking. Ms. Cuss-everybody-out-in-the-police-station!

DOTTY. No I didn't!

SHELLY. Yes you did!

DOTTY. No I didn't!

SHELLY. *(To* **JACKIE**.*)* Yes, she did.

DOTTY. We should be a good example to little Jason. He is very impressionable at his young age.

JACKIE. I *really* can come back later. I just needed to borrow a few things, Mrs. Shealy. I can come back later, I can come back later!

DOTTY. What do you need Jackie?

JACKIE. Well I just wanted to borrow a few things. Linen, lightbulbs, things like that.

DOTTY. That's not a problem.

JACKIE. Thank you.

DOTTY. I almost forgot what you looked like!

JACKIE. I changed my hair.

DOTTY. So did this one.

JACKIE. Blonde!

SHELLY. Something different.

DOTTY. You used to be down here all the time for a meal and our little talks.

SHELLY. Talks?

JACKIE. Yeah.

SHELLY. What talks?

DOTTY. None of yo business talks.

JACKIE. Nothing really.

DOTTY. Did you find my tape recorder Shelly?

SHELLY. *(Looking in the cabinet.)* What? Shit –

DOTTY. Language // my tape recorder.

SHELLY. // Mom did you move things around in these cabinets since yesterday?

DOTTY. What? No!

SHELLY. Yes you did!

DOTTY. No, I didn't.

SHELLY. Yes, she did.

JACKIE. *(Changing the subject.)* Um… Harlem has changed a lot probably since the last time you were there. It is pretty clean now. There's even a brand-new Whole Foods a couple of blocks away!

DOTTY. Our neighborhood has just gone down. Hmph, Democrats.

SHELLY. Mom, what are talking about? You're a Democrat!

DOTTY. I know, I know, but when I was coming up it was all turned around. Democrats were Republicans and Republicans were Democrats. *(To SHELLY.)* Move – I got it.

SHELLY. Mom –

DOTTY. I got it! I want mushrooms in mine.

> (DOTTY *gets up from the table and goes into the fridge and brings out some mushrooms.*)

SHELLY. Fine.

> (SHELLY *sits and pulls out her cell phone to make a call.* DOTTY *cooks her eggs. She is as serious as a heart attack about what she remembers.*)

DOTTY. The Republicans were the ones that ended slavery and looked after front stoops. I don't remember when it happened, but it looked like the only people that looked after one another were the Democrats. Jimmy Carter and them.

SHELLY. I know Mom, you campaigned for every primary since // 1960!

DOTTY. // 1960! People took care of the front steps and put out potted plants that would line the stoop. When we moved in here in the fifties, we were some of the first few blacks in this neighborhood! *(Continued to next speech.)*

SHELLY. *(To* JACKIE, *sarcastically.)* Does my brother pick up the phone for you?

JACKIE. Um, what? I haven't spoken to him in awhile.

SHELLY. Tell it to the Mayor! I know, I know. You told it to the Mayor. She told it to the Mayor. She was the

block captain remember? *(Beat.)* When she goes in
on something these days she goes all the way in. Or
completely OUT!

JACKIE. I don't understand. What do you mean by OUT?
What's going on?

DOTTY. *(Leaving the eggs cooking on the stove.)* // Mayor
Joseph Clark. One of them good white men. Even had
a TV show, called *Tell it to the Mayor*! So the people
could "tell it to the Mayor" on TV. And I "told it to
the Mayor" a couple of times. Asked questions about
sanitation and summer kids programs. I was the block
captain and I was responsible for the summer lunch
program. As working class people we depended on
breakfast and lunch being served in school. Remember
Shelly? I had you going in at seven a.m. to get that
breakfast? Cock a doodle doo!

SHELLY. Yes. Powdered eggs.

DOTTY. Probably like how mine are right now.

JACKIE. I'm sorry?

DOTTY. Ain't nothing but powdered eggs down below,
Marlo.

SHELLY. MOM!

DOTTY. What?

SHELLY. That's Jackie.

DOTTY. That's what I said, Jackie.

SHELLY. No, you didn't you called her Ms. Marlo!

DOTTY. What was I talking about?

JACKIE. Uh, well, *Tell it to the Mayor*?

DOTTY. Why?

SHELLY. *(Noticing the eggs left cooking on the stove.* **SHELLY**
*dumps burnt eggs into garbage and proceeds with making a
new plate of eggs.)* I have no idea! // Mom – shit –

DOTTY. // I loved that show. I was on there plenty of times.
Tell it to the Mayor. I would wear my finest June Cleaver
dress and pearls. //

SHELLY. // How many times are you going to tell this
story? Oh, one more time? Okay.

DOTTY. // Well not real pearls, costume jewelry. The Mayor wasn't ready for me, with my keen insight on how to solve the problems of the inner city. I threw out rumination on how to get women involved in all forms of neighborhood associations because as I've always told you girls...

DOTTY, SHELLY, JACKIE. Women are the ones who really get things done.

JACKIE. At least we try. I'm trying.

DOTTY. I was a feminist before there was a word for it. Without women, there is no life. We are the titty of the world!

SHELLY. // OK, that's enough!

JACKIE. // Is that coffee in that cup, Mrs. Shealy?

DOTTY. All I'm saying is, I'm from people who struggled to get a little piece of something. Now that that little something is so easy to get, no one cares about stoops and potted plants. Sheila down the street drives a – what is that Shelly?

SHELLY. A Range Rover.

DOTTY. And keeps her porch filled with garbage cans and niggas.

JACKIE. Oh, wow –

SHELLY. MOM!

DOTTY. You know what they are –

SHELLY. MOM, eat your eggs!

(**SHELLY** *puts the eggs down in front of* **DOTTY**.)

DOTTY. She don't like it when I talk about these niggas!

SHELLY. MOM, I'm not playing with you! Eat your eggs!

DOTTY. I'm eating them, I'm eating them!

(**DOTTY** *eats the eggs.*)

SHELLY. Oh my God! *(To* **JACKIE**.*)* So what do you need?

DOTTY. They are niggas! That is what niggas do! Ride around in Range Rovers and don't take care of their front stoops!

SHELLY. Eat Mom! I don't have time for this! I have to go back to the hairdresser and then pick up the tree if you want a real tree.

DOTTY. I was wondering what was going on with your hair. You look like a mean pineapple.

SHELLY. Don't mess with me. I will go to the basement and pull out Daddy's hot pink artificial tree like I want to.

DOTTY. No, no, no, I want a Spruce!

SHELLY. Then let's get the jokes in check!

DOTTY. A Blue Spruce! I got to have a Blue Spruce. Like my daddy used to get! Used to cut it down with his own two hands. Like Paul Bunyan! Jackie, chile, I ain't had a real tree in years!

JACKIE. Neither have I, Mrs. Shealy.

SHELLY. Then let's leave the hair alone.

DOTTY. I'll leave it alone, I'll leave it alone. It's just brassy, is all I'm sayin'.

SHELLY. I know, I know, I know. It's too brassy.

JACKIE. You always wore your hair long with a perm. Why did you cut it so short?

SHELLY. When I am stressed out, I tell Andre to give me something different.

DOTTY. Why are all hairdressers named Andre?

SHELLY. If you ask me one more question I'm gonna light myself on fire.

DOTTY. (Laughs.) It's brassy. She looks like a mean pineapple.

SHELLY. You said that! Wasn't funny a minute ago. EAT! They must have made this Watermelon Vodka just for me.

DOTTY. Why you drinkin' so early in the day?

SHELLY. I am grown! I can drink when the rooster crows if I feel like it.

DOTTY. What a mouth! I don't know where you got a mouth like that.

SHELLY. Apple doesn't fall far from the tree.

DOTTY. And what you talking bout roosters crowing? This is the city. Ain't no roosters –

SHELLY. MOM! *(Referring to a cocktail.)* You sure you don't want one?

JACKIE. No, Shelly, I'm fine. I *really* should –

DOTTY. Jackie, do you talk to your mother this way?

JACKIE. No.

SHELLY. Well, that would be a miracle! Being as though Ms. Marlo has been dead for years.

DOTTY. That's not what I meant. Shelly can you get Jackie some sheets and things from the linen closet? I'm going to the market.

> *(**DOTTY** looks for her keys.)*

SHELLY. No you're not, Mom.

JACKIE. And can I borrow some sweats?

DOTTY. Shelly, don't you got somewhere to go and leave me the hell alone?

SHELLY. Well I do, but I don't and I won't. I have stuff to do around here.

DOTTY. So bossy.

SHELLY. Mom, you haven't finished your breakfast.

DOTTY. Food don't get in that fridge by itself.

SHELLY. I'll go with you later.

DOTTY. I can't find my keys.

SHELLY. Talk to her while I get you some linen. *(To **DOTTY**.)* Remember Ms. Marlo died?

> *(**SHELLY** goes upstairs to retrieve the linen and sweats.)*

DOTTY. Yes I remember! I remember. We sent all of those white roses.

JACKIE. Yes you did. Donnie picked them out.

DOTTY. Picked what out?

> *(**DOTTY** continues to search for her keys.)*

JACKIE. The roses. He knew that she loved those.

DOTTY. Yeah, he knew. Donnie knows. *(Beat.)* You got a cigarette?

JACKIE. A cigarette?

DOTTY. She hid mine. She hides everything.

JACKIE. I never knew you smoked.

DOTTY. There's a lot of things that you don't know about me. You got any weed?

JACKIE. Weed?

DOTTY. Yeah, weed.

JACKIE. Um…no. Mrs. Shealy. When did you start smoking weed?

DOTTY. Weed?

JACKIE. Yes, weed.

DOTTY. Where you been?

JACKIE. New York. Don't change the subject Mrs. Shealy. Since when do you smoke weed?

DOTTY. Everybody's doing it. Tiny, Boo, Dawn.

JACKIE. Who is Tiny, Boo and Dawn?

DOTTY. Where you been? Why haven't I seen you in so long.

JACKIE. No, Mrs. Shealy don't change the subject.

DOTTY. You changing the subject.

JACKIE. No, you are.

DOTTY. Am I?

JACKIE. Yes.

DOTTY. Where you been?

JACKIE. Um. Well, I – I – I just needed to get a little distance. Well, not from you, but, yes from the family. If I was ever going to expect to get a family of my own, I had to get a little distance, you know? Now back to Tiny, Boo and Dawn –

DOTTY. Just because Donnie is gay // doesn't mean that you are not a part of this family.

JACKIE. // I don't think me hanging around here was very healthy for me –

(**SHELLY** *returns with the linen and sweats.*)

SHELLY. Sheets, blanket and the only sweats I could find were some of Donnie's old sweats from his track and field days.

JACKIE. Okay, thank you. Thank you.

SHELLY. Not a problem. If you are not going to rent out that old house, when are you going to let it go?

JACKIE. Um…never! Only child. Dead parents. Something to hold on to.

SHELLY. It's empty.

JACKIE. It's home.

DOTTY. What time is it?

SHELLY. Mom? It's ten o'clock. Eat please. And take your medication.

JACKIE. What's going on. You asked that a few times now, Mrs. Shealy. Shelly what's going on?

SHELLY. Ask her.

DOTTY. Ask me what?

JACKIE. Are you alright, Mrs. Shealy?

DOTTY. I just need salt. (*She gets up to go search the cabinet.*)

SHELLY. Mom, you can't have salt!

DOTTY. It needs something. You can't expect me to give up everything? I need salt.

SHELLY. Go ahead then. Have salt! Kill yourself!

DOTTY. I just need salt!

(**DOTTY** *searches the cabinets.*)

SHELLY. She apparently NEEDS salt.

JACKIE. Shelly, I should go. I don't know what is going on and it's probably not my business so I will let you guys work out whatever you need to work out. I have to pick up a few things.

SHELLY. Just give me a minute. How long you staying?

JACKIE. I'm not really sure.

SHELLY. What do you have to pick up?

JACKIE. I came down here in the spur of the moment.

SHELLY. I knew it! Spill the tea.

> (**DOTTY** *returns from the cabinets with Oreo cookies.*)

DOTTY. Good ole Jackie! How you doing? You still living in New York?

JACKIE. Um… Yes! Mrs. Shealy. I am still living in New York.

SHELLY. Mom, you left the cabinets open again.

DOTTY. Where?

JACKIE. I told you, Harlem.

DOTTY. Is it still dirty?

SHELLY. Mom, you asked her that.

DOTTY. Asked her what?

SHELLY. Is New York still dirty.

DOTTY. I did?

SHELLY. Yes, you did. Why you got Oreos? Where's the salt?

DOTTY. The salt?

SHELLY. The salt.

DOTTY. The salt?

SHELLY. Mom, you wanted salt and you got Oreos.

JACKIE. It's okay Shelly.

SHELLY. *(Emotionally cracks.)* NO, IT'S NOT OKAY! THESE ARE OREOS AND SHE WANTED SALT!

> *(Dead silence.)*

JACKIE. *(Soberly.)* What the fuck is going on?

> *(Silence.)*
>
> *(Silence.)*
>
> *(Silence.)*

Mrs. Shealy? *(Beat.)* Shelly?

SHELLY. You gonna tell her?

DOTTY. Tell her what?

JACKIE. Tell me what?

SHELLY. About… Don't make me do this. It's something that your doctor said // that YOU should share.

JACKIE. // Doctor? Oh my God. What is it? What is it?

DOTTY. I'm fine, I'm fine, my daughter is being overly dramatic.

SHELLY. Mom?

DOTTY. I got some memory problems.

SHELLY. Mom?

DOTTY. Just forgetful. Getting old.

SHELLY. MOM?

DOTTY. I get confused sometimes.

SHELLY. Mom tell her.

JACKIE. Tell me what? What? What is it?

DOTTY. What day is this?

JACKIE. Tuesday.

DOTTY. Tuesday.

SHELLY. See?

DOTTY. See what?

JACKIE. What?

DOTTY. Two days 'til Christmas. Tuesday. I got to find my tape recorder. I gotta tape some things for little Jason. What time is –

SHELLY. Mom, please, ten, ten, TEN!

DOTTY. Can I use the bathroom officer?

SHELLY. You don't have to ask me to use the bathroom.

DOTTY. My daughter is like a Marine. She got it from her father.

SHELLY. Mom. Grandad was in the Marines.

DOTTY. You know who I'm talking about!

SHELLY. Just go, Mom.

DOTTY. *(She salutes.)* YES SIR!

>   (**DOTTY** *exits into the bathroom.*)
>   (*Silence.*)

JACKIE. Shelly what's going on –

SHELLY. Ssh. Just give me a…minute.

> (**SHELLY** *picks up the rotary phone on the wall to call* **DONNIE**. *He doesn't answer. She bangs the receiver several times like a mad woman.*)
>
> *(Silence.)*
>
> *(Silence.)*
>
> *(Silence.)*

JACKIE. Shelly, you guys still have a rotary –

SHELLY. *(She takes a quick drink of vodka.)* Okay. I'm good. *(Beat.)* It's dementia.

JACKIE. Oh my God!

SHELLY. Yeah. Alzheimer's. It's a bitch.

JACKIE. Oh my God, Oh my God. Oh my God!

SHELLY. Yeah.

JACKIE. How long has this been going on?

SHELLY. She was diagnosed, what, about a year ago?

JACKIE. A year ago?

SHELLY. A year ago!

JACKIE. Oh Shelly, I am so sorry.

SHELLY. We think that she was hiding it from us for a while. Probably hiding it from herself.

JACKIE. I am so sorry.

SHELLY. It's alright. You didn't do it. Last fall I got a call from the cops that she got pulled over for driving ninety-five miles an hour –

JACKIE. // Ninety-five miles an hour?

SHELLY. Yup. On Wissahickon Drive.

JACKIE. Around all those curves and bends?

SHELLY. Right where Teddy Pendergrass crashed his car with that transsexual –

JACKIE. I know the spot –

SHELLY. And when the cop asked why she was driving so fast, she said that "the wind felt good on her" –

JACKIE. Oh, Shelly.

SHELLY. The cop asked where she was going and she didn't know. She had no idea where she was going. Found my number as one of the last numbers dialed in her phone and called me –

JACKIE. Thank God for cell phone recall –

SHELLY. I came and picked her up from the police station down on Girard Avenue. Now you know, I do not go down on Girard Avenue. Chile… It was such a scene. I'm trying to verify that she is my mother and then she freaked out and cussed EVERYBODY out and they had the paramedics take her to the hospital and deal with all THAT and then they kept her for a few days and did all of these tests and then the questions about her health and sanity and well, you know…

JACKIE. Shelly, I'm so sorry.

SHELLY. I can't let her be in this house alone.

JACKIE. You can't leave her alone?

SHELLY. Hell NO! Not unless I put her to bed. I am afraid of what she will get into or forget to do. Give her a mild sleeping aid and I'm good.

JACKIE. Perhaps you should look into other alternatives.

SHELLY. I'm doing what I can. I take one too. It's over the counter, something I got in Paris a few years ago. It's all good.

JACKIE. Okay. As long as you are keeping that in check.

SHELLY. For the past few weeks, I've had to take her with me to work. On Friday, she drove me so crazy trying to organize my files at my office. Said she was trying to help. I come in from a staff meeting and she is pointing to a crazy looking file, telling me to take a hard look at it.

JACKIE. What was it?

SHELLY. Something she made with newspaper articles and a whole lot of random chaos. One minute she is so lucid, remembering names of mayors of the 1950s and the next, she doesn't remember what she asked one

minute ago. On Halloween I think she told me that she
planned on killing herself.

JACKIE. No, oh my God!

SHELLY. Well not in those words. She said, "I don't ever
want to be a burden to anyone. I will go when I am in
control of it! I won't linger and be a burden."

JACKIE. Oh my God!

SHELLY. The way her mind works, she probably forgot she
said that. But you can't be too sure. So I'm watching.
(Beat.) It has been me and her locked in my office on
the days when Fidel // is not here to be with her.

JACKIE. // Who is Fidel?

SHELLY. This boy that I hired off of Craigslist. He is not a
certified nurse but he has a lot of experience taking
care of the elderly. He is from Kazakhstan.

JACKIE. Kazakhstan? What is that?

SHELLY. Former Soviet Union. He and my mother seem to
have a little bond going. Looking like they are plotting
at times. Communicating in their own crazy way with
nods and stares. He comes in cleans, cooks, does
laundry, makes sure that the house is not burned down
two to three times a week and I pay him fifty dollars a
day.

JACKIE. That's good. Can he be here full time?

SHELLY. With all my own expenses that is the best that I can
do until I get my hands on my brother and sister. It is
long overdue for them to take over some responsibility.
She's going to need full time care, like, YESTERDAY.

JACKIE. Funny thing is that she looks fine.

SHELLY. And I look like a mean pineapple.

JACKIE. You just need to soften it. Is there anything I can –

SHELLY. I look like a dyke, don't I?

JACKIE. No, you don't look like a dyke. Shelly –

SHELLY. My son said I looked like his teacher's partner,
Ms. Woods.

JACKIE. His teacher is a lesbian?

SHELLY. It's a Quaker school. Ms. Woods is a big old knuckle dragging bull dagger.

JACKIE. Really?

SHELLY. Now you know I ain't got no problem with lesbians. I was one for a few months in college.

JACKIE. Weren't we all?

SHELLY. But Ms. Woods is a man! When I asked Jason, how did my haircut look and he said like Ms. Woods, my knees buckled, my eyes rolled to the back of my head and I almost passed out, right here in the kitchen with *Spongebob* playing in the background.

JACKIE. It actually looks more like Spongebob's cut.

SHELLY. *(Sotto voce.)* Whatchu doin' here?

JACKIE. For a visit. I just decided to come home for a while.

SHELLY. Girl, no one comes to this neighborhood for a visit. A funeral maybe, but not a visit.

JACKIE. Why can't I just visit? I haven't been here in what?

SHELLY. Let's see…two years ago. Since you popped over here and ran into Donnie and Adam cuddled up on the couch?

JACKIE. Really?

SHELLY. Mmm-hmm.

JACKIE. Don't people just drop in to say hello to the old neighborhood?

SHELLY. NO.

JACKIE. Sometimes!

SHELLY. No they don't.

JACKIE. Yes, they do!

SHELLY. Get to it!

JACKIE. I'm pregnant!

SHELLY. Shut up!

JACKIE. Eight weeks.

SHELLY. Shut up!

JACKIE. By a man that ain't mine.

SHELLY. SHUT. UP.

JACKIE. He's got a wife and kids –

SHELLY. And a chick that is knocked up!

JACKIE. I know. Ssh, be quiet. I feel terrible. I don't know how I got in this situation. I feel awful.

SHELLY. You should… Huzzy.

JACKIE. I QUIT! QUIT! I think I quit my JOB and NEW YORK, as I did leave right in the middle of a wedding that we were catering at the Waldorf Astoria. Watching these two people who looked so in love and so happy. They looked right out of those magazines like *Brides*! I HATED them. I wanted to EXPLODE! I was a Molotov cocktail ready to be thrown into the fray of bliss! They suddenly shoved my life in my face. The YEARS of living in the BIG CITY with BIG DREAMS and thinking I was Carrie Bradshaw or Samantha or some shit. Dating what available men there were in New York and FAILING miserably and hoping HOPING and BELIEVING that my prince charming would come, like every little girl, but then the YEARS tick tock and then you look up and you're FORTY and the only men trying to holler at you are married or fucked up or a creep, because a bunch of BITCHES already got dibs on the good men that you let slip through your fingers because you hated the way they chewed their food or something else insignificant and just that morning you went to the doctor and found out that you were eight weeks pregnant a couple of days after the white stick turned blue and you look over in the middle of the wedding and see the smug married asshole whose side piece you have been for a year and a half, and turn back to the happy bride in Vera Wang and her Don Draper-looking husband and you just decide to GIDDYAPP and leave in the middle of the "I do's" and hightail it through the Lincoln Tunnel as if you have a SCARLET LETTER tattooed on your forehead – I just had to come home – that is all I could think about – to get my head together and re-evaluate my so-called

LIFE! I got a MESS of a life. A MESS OF A LIFE! Just gimme a sip of that Watermelon Vodka.

SHELLY. A sip.

(*JACKIE downs a few sips.*)

A sip! All you need is for that baby to come out with three heads.

JACKIE. New York can just be TOO MUCH. You know what I mean? The pace of it all. And I got caught up in the pace. Caught up with Gilberto. That's his name.

SHELLY. Of course it is.

JACKIE. Gilberto San Jose. He owns the event company that I manage. You know me, I am always so busy and he was just… THERE. It's good to be home. Home.

SHELLY. You're a smart girl. You will figure it out. MOM WHATCHU DOING IN THERE?

JACKIE. Life was so easy before we became adults! If your brother just kept his promise, I wouldn't be in this mess.

SHELLY. No, you'd be in ANOTHER mess! He's as gay as giftwrap.

JACKIE. True, true. How is Donnie?

SHELLY. Getting on my nerves. The Golden Boy // will be here tomorrow with his husband.

JACKIE. // You still call him that? Adam right?

SHELLY. Yes, Adam. They got married.

JACKIE. This summer. I know.

SHELLY. I know you know. You didn't show. MOM YOU DONE?

JACKIE. I was out of the country.

SHELLY. You suddenly had to go to Mexico. I watch your Twitter feed girl. You planned that trip in twenty-four hours.

JACKIE. Shelly, I couldn't.

SHELLY. I wasn't going to bring it up. He was hurt but I thought that was your business. MOM?

DOTTY. *(Offstage.)* I'm doing my business!

SHELLY. *(To* **DOTTY.***)* GOOD! DON'T FALL IN! *(To* **JACKIE.***)* We got a few more minutes.

JACKIE. I just didn't want to make Adam uncomfortable. Donnie and I were a couple. I didn't want to be a threat.

SHELLY. You were not going to be a threat to anybody! It was FIRE ISLAND! Gay Disney with booze! Wasn't nobody thinking about you! He and Adam got married on the beach and everybody wore white. Jason is nine and he loved it. Kids these days benefit from exposure.

JACKIE. That's nice. That's really good for them. I wish them the best.

SHELLY. You still carrying that flame.

JACKIE. Of course not. We were teenagers. *(Tsk.)* Flame.

SHELLY. You turned him gay.

JACKIE. No I didn't and you don't turn anyone gay.

SHELLY. You did!

JACKIE. I didn't.

SHELLY. You were his last girlfriend and then POOF!

JACKIE. You really think you are funny.

SHELLY. You still need to work things through with him. It's been what? Twenty years now.

JACKIE. I don't need to work ANYTHING out! I've worked it out! *(Tsk.)* Flame.

SHELLY. I don't even want to talk about him right now because his ass is on my last. He hasn't returned my calls in about three weeks. **(SHELLY** *removes the trash from the bin.)* All he does is text. I got too much to say that requires picking up a phone instead of texting. He and Averie both! Donnie needs to give up on that newspaper career and get a real job and Averie needs to do a little better than working BACK down at the "PRICERIGHT"! Because they both have to help out in a big way and that requires adult strategies. Am I right?

JACKIE. Preach!

SHELLY. Who am I talking to? You are on the run with a bun in the oven.

(**SHELLY** *takes the trash outside.*)

JACKIE. You got me. Guilty as charged. But wait, doesn't Donnie make a good income? He writes for newspapers and magazines.

SHELLY. That is a thing of the past! You know nobody is reading those things anymore. I don't remember the last time I read a newspaper, period. (**SHELLY** *re-enters, shuts door.*) I get my news online.

JACKIE. Same here.

SHELLY. And his husband is working for some Rainbow Alliance or something or other. NON-PROFIT which equals NO MONEY!

JACKIE. Oh okay. I see. But what about Averie? Didn't she make a lot of money from being a YouTube sensation?

SHELLY. GONE! I told her to put all that money away that she got from all those interviews and appearances at clubs. But you know that term "Nigga Rich"? Hmph! That's what I'm saying. She's living in my basement.

JACKIE. Oh, I thought you were living here again.

SHELLY. No, but I am here most of the time. It's a good thing because Averie is a lot!

JACKIE. She had those commercials running –

SHELLY. I don't consider a 1-800-Bad-Credit or a 555-We-Do-Hair, legitimate commercials. She had the nerve to get herself an agent and a manager. Actually – they came after her! Agents and managers! Agenting and managing WHAT?! She was suddenly a celebrity! Ain't that some shit? Hmph, these bootleg people that she had running her newfound career took most of her money and now she is back at the "PRICERIGHT," cashiering.

JACKIE. Well that's good. She's got a job!

(**SHELLY** *shoots* **JACKIE** *a look of death.*)

Don't hate me, but I played that YouTube clip of her chasing down that pick pocket and getting that old lady's purse back like a hundred times.

SHELLY. Caught on a cell phone.

SHELLY & JACKIE. "You would rather run through hell in kerosene-soaked draws than to raise your hand at me!"

SHELLY. She is a walking lexicon of street slang. Well, she ain't got a thin dime now. But she and my brother are going to have to get some money together so we can get Mom some permanent care because I am going berserk! *(Beat.)* I sound like such a bitch. Girl, I don't feel like myself. This isn't me. I'm fun. Fun! Right?

> *(Silence.)*

JACKIE. It's the holidays. Everyone is just a bit more wound up. *(Sincerely.)* You're fun.

SHELLY. I'm a bitch.

JACKIE. No, you're not.

SHELLY. Yes I am. I feel TIGHT. TIGHT ALL OVER. All the time. Which is why I'm drinking in the morning.

JACKIE. You just have a lot going on. Hey, I'll join you.

SHELLY. Join what?

JACKIE. Can you make me a Watermelon Vodka drink thing?

SHELLY. You want a cigarette, too? What is this, the 1950s? You're pregnant! NO!

JACKIE. But, wait, I don't know if I'm keeping it.

SHELLY. Well then, NO, until you figure it out!

JACKIE. Fine. Fine. *(Beat.)* I just need a moment to regroup and think about what this single, forty-year-old Jewish woman is going to do. Oy vey.

SHELLY. Who's Jewish?

JACKIE. Me!

SHELLY. Since when?

JACKIE. Um, FOREVER.

SHELLY. And you think you know somebody. JEWISH! I just always thought you were the white girl whose family didn't run out of this neighborhood in the white flight of the seventies.

JACKIE. Not my Jewish hippie parents. Unh unh!

SHELLY. Back when we were Afro-American! You still trying to pass?

JACKIE. I had those cornrows once!

SHELLY. I don't care how many white girls come back from Jamaica with their hair cornrowed! You ain't fooling nobody girl!

JACKIE. *(Laughing.)* I wasn't trying to pass, I just wanted to have black hair. You can do so much with it!
Watching Roland Chambers part and grease your hair!

SHELLY. Roland played me like he played those drums for Philly International. Banged the –

> *(**DOTTY** comes out of the bathroom. **SHELLY** and **JACKIE** do not see her. She just stands there looking confused about whether she went to the bathroom or not.)*

JACKIE. When I am in that house I can put my hand on my old bedroom wall and feel all that history. That music. If am going to have a child, I would want that child to have all that soul. Right here.

SHELLY. *(Lost in a sexual memory.)* Hmph. Roland.

> *(**DOTTY** exits back into the bathroom.)*

JACKIE. Listen, I know. I wasn't smart.

SHELLY. Nope! But, I'm not going to judge you.

JACKIE. Sounds like judgment but okay, thank you.

SHELLY. You're welcome.

JACKIE. I told you too much. Please don't tell anybody. Oh my God, I hope your mom hasn't heard any of this.

SHELLY. If she did, she won't remember.

JACKIE. Really?

SHELLY. It's Alzheimer's. Mom? You alright? I'mma have to go in there in a minute if she doesn't come out.

JACKIE. I'm sorry for dumping my shit on you. My problems seem so insignificant compared to Alzhei… *(Beat.)* These are things I can at least control in one way or another. Although I have no idea what I am doing.

SHELLY. Honestly, neither do I. I'm just trying to keep us afloat.

(**SHELLY** *shows* **JACKIE** *a very nice brochure.*)

(Sotto voce.) I found a pretty good assisted living community out on City Line Avenue. *(She checks on the folder that she asked* **DOTTY** *to sign earlier.)* And thankfully I got her to sign for me to get power of attorney so I can make this shit happen if she slips into a more deteriorated state. I can't wait for any other plan. Fidel is all I can afford right now – *(She realizes.)* SHIT! She didn't sign!

(**DOTTY** *enters.*)

DOTTY. Fidel is from Kazahkastan! Always on the SKYPES to call his mother since he doesn't have the internet where he lives.

SHELLY. MOM! You didn't sign! The power of attorney –

DOTTY. Oh really? What time is it?

SHELLY. Ten something! Okay! BEDTIME! Sign later!

DOTTY. At ten a.m.?

SHELLY. P.M.!

DOTTY. But it's still light out.

JACKIE. Shelly…

SHELLY. AURORA BOREALIS!

DOTTY. What?

SHELLY. THE NORTHERN LIGHTS.

DOTTY. In West Philly?

SHELLY. GLOBAL WARMING.

DOTTY. But I'm about to have my breakfast!

SHELLY. You already had it for dessert! Let's get you to bed.

DOTTY. Well…goodnight everybody!

SHELLY. Goodnight.

DOTTY. I'm not even tired.

SHELLY. I am.

DOTTY. When are you going to take care of that brassy hair?

SHELLY. Tomorrow. Come on, MOM, BRUSH YOUR TEETH AND TUCK YOURSELF IN!

DOTTY. SHELLY! STOP TREATING ME LIKE A CHILD! I AM YOUR MOTHER!

> *(Silence.)*
>
> *(Silence.)*
>
> *(Silence.)*

It's Christmas in a few days.

SHELLY. I know, I'm picking up your tree.

DOTTY. What do you want for Christmas?

SHELLY. Nothing Mom, I don't want anything.

DOTTY. Everybody wants something.

SHELLY. Mom, I don't need anything.

DOTTY. What do you want Jackie?

> *(***JACKIE** *bursts into tears.)*

You alright?

JACKIE. I'm fine Mrs. Shealy. My emotions are just all over the place. Christmas coming and all.

DOTTY. You look pregnant.

JACKIE. I'm just a little overwhelmed that's all.

DOTTY. And pregnant. Mark my words. You might wanna get one of them little box tests. Shelly you got any?

SHELLY. What?

DOTTY. You and Averie used to keep a whole case of 'em under your bed.

SHELLY. Goodnight!

DOTTY. Your sense of humor must have been burned out with that hair color!

SHELLY. I'm about to be on the news tonight Jackie!

DOTTY. *(She sees the tape recorder on the fridge and takes it.)* The boys are coming in tonight, right?

SHELLY. Yes. Tonight. LATE. Your boys are coming in late tonight. Donnie said that he and Adam can't come in until about midnight. You will see them in the morning. Them and the Blue Spruce!

DOTTY. I'll wake up to a Blue Spruce on Christmas Eve morning.
Goodnight.

SHELLY. Goodnight.

DOTTY. Love you, Pookie.

SHELLEY. I love you more.

DOTTY. *(To* **JACKIE**.*)* Goodnight.

JACKIE. Uh. Goodnight?

> *(***DOTTY** *goes up the stairs.)*

Aurora Borealis?

SHELLY. AURORA BOREALIS! You're lucky! Your mother's gone already! Mine is here and gone at the same time! AURORA BOREALIS! I gotta go pick up a Blue Spruce, take care of this brassy ass hair and get ready for Christmas!

> *("I'LL LET YOU KNOW" by David Hazeltine plays.**
> *Jazz.* **SHELLY** *exits.* **JACKIE** *collects her belongings*
> *and exits. Snow falls. The kitchen light goes dim.*
> *Lights shift. Late at night.)*

---

* A license to produce *Dot* does not include a performance license for "I'll Let You Know." Please see Music Use Note on page 3 for further information.

A DETOX

*(**DONNIE**, forty, African American, handsome, masculine, and fit, is sneaking into the kitchen. He wears J.Crew loungewear. Opens a cabinet. Reaches to the far back. Retrieves oatmeal cookies. Gorges. Goes to fridge. Pulls out lemonade from the fridge. Drinks heartily. Pulls fried chicken from the fridge. Closes fridge. Footsteps. He shoves everything in the fridge. Pulls out a glass and fills with water. **ADAM**, forty, Caucasian, buff specimen of a man, suddenly appears. **DONNIE** is almost caught in the act! AHA!)*

ADAM. What are you doing?

DONNIE. Water.

ADAM. There were a lot of cabinet openings and closings for water.

DONNIE. I was looking for an Advil.

ADAM. Come here.

(They begin to circle the kitchen table.)

DONNIE. Why?

ADAM. I wanna kiss.

DONNIE. No.

ADAM. Why?

DONNIE. I don't feel like it. It's late. My breath stinks.

ADAM. Like what?

DONNIE. I don't know, like stink.

ADAM. Like food of some sort. I swear –

(They stop circling.)

DONNIE. No.
   No! Really. No.

ADAM. Because we are on day four of the juice cleanse, *(They start circling the kitchen table again.)* it would be a shame if you didn't follow through.

DONNIE. That shit is expensive, of course I'm following through.

ADAM. We have just one more day and then we need transitional raw and vegan meals.

DONNIE. Whose idea was it to do a juice cleanse before the holidays.

ADAM. Yours.

DONNIE. I just put it on the calendar. I forgot what day it was.

ADAM. How can you forget five days before Christmas?

DONNIE. People forget. I forgot.

ADAM. You forgot?

DONNIE. Anyway, I know, we are going to feel so much better. Right? This is great! Yesterday was rough but today I... I feel good. How do you feel? *(They stop circling.)*

ADAM. I feel good.

(**ADAM** *looks at* **DONNIE***'s stomach.*)

DONNIE. What?

ADAM. Nothing.

DONNIE. Am I too fat for you?

ADAM. What?

DONNIE. This "fast"?

ADAM. Come on! It's about staying healthy.

DONNIE. Oh really? Tell Molly.

ADAM. I TRIED IT ONCE!

DONNIE. YEAH, ON OUR WEDDING NIGHT!

ADAM. I haven't done it since. Get over it. What the fuck?

DONNIE. Really? What about Vann and George?

ADAM. I don't know if they do? OK, yeah, I'm sure they do.

DONNIE. Right.

ADAM. But this is me. Come on, I'm tired of this, give me a kiss.

DONNIE. Oh. What? Is it gonna lead to sex? I forgot what that was.

ADAM. OK. I think this fast is getting the better of you. What the fuck are you talking about? We had sex LAST MONTH!

DONNIE. Make-up sex.

ADAM. I guess NOT!

DONNIE. Well…somebody was a little too drunk to –

ADAM. Hey, not here.

DONNIE. Well, we don't talk at home.

ADAM. Well, you know what? It's hard to have sex with someone who is always so fucking angry and negative.

DONNIE. I'm negative?

ADAM. You are just so angry all of the time!

DONNIE. Do you read the news? This is America. I have EVERY FUCKING RIGHT TO BE ANGRY ALL OF THE TIME.

ADAM. I know. I know. We all do. I'm angry. But remember? We have to find the light. Remember the light?

DONNIE. Yeah, I remember the light. I'm trying. I'm trying.

(*Silence.*)

ADAM. Okay. (*Beat.*) I'm going back up. Come on.

(**ADAM** *starts to exit.*)

DONNIE. Why didn't you hold my hand?

ADAM. What?

DONNIE. When we were at your "*friend*" Robert's Christmas party last night?

ADAM. Why do you say it like that? "*Friend.*"

DONNIE. I hate those guys. Those circuit boy queens that live from one party to the next.

ADAM. They like to have FUN. So what? Is it a crime to have FUN?

DONNIE. Dressing alike in those high top sneakers and tank tops, backwards baseball caps // and look down on gays that are not clones just like them and have no idea of the history of who stonewalled for them! Cackling like little girls who think life is just one big sex, Andrew Christian, and Molly buffet. //

ADAM. // You know, I'm not going to listen to you bitch about my friends. *(Beat.)* Maybe if you got your head out of your writing and got some "friends" of your own you'd feel a little better. And stop being so insecure. Acting like an OLD MAN! Is that why you are still wound up? // The Molly? I tried it once! ONCE!

DONNIE. All you did was criticize the way I did things or the way I was dressed.

ADAM. You were way too dressed up!

DONNIE. We shouldn't have come.

> *(Silence.)*
>
> *(Silence.)*
>
> *(Silence.)*

ADAM. Mom's not –

...We need to be here with our family. It's Christmas. Christmas at the Shealy's.

> **(ADAM** *tries to reach out to* **DONNIE. DONNIE** *retreats.)*

You know I don't like going to sleep mad. Kiss me.

DONNIE. *(He tries to subtly check his breath.)* I don't feel like it.

ADAM. Do you not want to make things better? Kiss me. Kiss me gatdamnit!

> **(DOTTY** *enters.)*

DOTTY. Kiss him!

ADAM. Momma Dotty!

DONNIE. Mom!

DOTTY. Momma's sweet thangs! Give me a kiss!

> **(ADAM** *does.)*

ADAM. Give mommy a kiss! *(Whispers.)* Smell his breath.

DONNIE. NO.

DOTTY. Been in the cookie jar, hunh?

DONNIE. No!

DOTTY. You puttin' on a little weight!

DONNIE. I haven't seen you in months and this is the first thing out of your mouth?

DOTTY. Adam, what are you feeding my boy?

ADAM. I'm not feeding him anything.

DONNIE. I'm on a cleanse.

DOTTY. A what?

ADAM. A juice cleanse.

DOTTY. What in the world are you gays doing now? Why can't you just put on chaps and call it a day?

ADAM. *(Laughs.)* Chaps? Mommy Dotty, you crazy.

DOTTY. I told you, that's the way I like my gays! Handlebar mustaches and chaps. I think that's sexy.

ADAM. I do too. Tell Donnie.

DOTTY. Y'all are way too conservative for my taste. Whatchu wearing, J.Crew or something? Come on now, if you gonna be gay, BE GAY! I think I got an old boa in the basement.

> (**DOTTY** *goes to the cabinets in search of a snack or tea or something. Pulls many things out and leaves them in disarray. She eventually settles for a bowl of nuts and takes them with her to the table.*)

ADAM. We only do that on Fire Island!

DOTTY. Fire Island! I love it! Are you getting that house in the Pines again next year?

ADAM. We are not going to get the house ever, EVER, again.

DOTTY. Why?

ADAM. Donnie –

DONNIE. Doesn't want to! What are you doing up Mom?

DOTTY. My sleep is all over the place. I don't know. Wait, wait, wait, I'm focused. Why aren't you gonna get the house? You get it every year. It's become your tradition. You gotta hold up your traditions.

DONNIE. I'm not doing it anymore! I don't need that tradition. Case closed!

DOTTY. Donnie what's wrong?

DONNIE. Nothing Mom, I'm just tired. It's late, we should all get some sleep.

DOTTY. I felt like I slept all night and day yesterday. That "Aurora Borealis."

(**DOTTY** *cracks the nuts.*)

ADAM. Aurora Borealis?

DOTTY. The Northern Lights.

DONNIE. The Northern Lights?

ADAM. The Northern Lights?

DOTTY. Shelly told me that –

ADAM. Here?

DONNIE. In West Philly?

DOTTY. The Northern Lights are now in West Philly. Global warming.

DONNIE. *(Sotto voce.)* Fuck. *(Shrieks.)* Shelly!

ADAM. Donnie.

DOTTY. Son, why are you yelling at three o'clock in the morning?

DONNIE. *(Whispering to **ADAM**.)* I'm gonna kill her. She had her sleeping all day again.

ADAM. *(Whispering.)* What's that smell on your breath? Smells like chicken and cookies.

DONNIE. What?

ADAM. Chicken and cookies.

DONNIE. *(Yelling.)* SHELLY?!

(**SHELLY** *comes into the kitchen. Her hair color is now red.*)

SHELLY. What's wrong with you? Why are you shrieking my name?

DOTTY. Don't y'all get started. It's almost Christmas Eve. Why is your hair red?

SHELLY. Leave it alone. Why is all this stuff out here?

DOTTY. It seems like, every time I go to sleep, I wake up and you have another hair color!

SHELLY. It was too brassy, remember?

DONNIE. You got her sleeping all day again?

SHELLY. Yes I do. I'm stressed! I got my hair colored but the queen fucked it up. I ain't going to him no more.

DONNIE. *(Sotto voce.)* Answer me! Why you got Mom sleeping all day?

SHELLY. *(Sotto voce.)* Why you worried about it? You ain't here! Hey Adam. You looking buffed up. You been working out?

ADAM. I have. Thank you for noticing. I like the red! Very Jessica Rabbit.

SHELLY. Thank you! I had a do-over.

ADAM. Looks good. I'm sorry, are we too loud? Where's Jason?

SHELLY. Sleepover.

DOTTY. Who was sleeping all day?

SHELLY. NOBODY!

DONNIE. *(Sotto voce.)* I thought you said that it was only for emergencies.

SHELLY. *(Sotto voce.)* Everyday is an emergency.

DONNIE. She's fine.

DOTTY. Shelly did you get the tree?

SHELLY. I got it mom, I got it! I "Paul Bunyan-ed" it. It's in there.

DOTTY. Yes Lord!

> (**DOTTY** *goes into the living room with* **ADAM** *on her heels.*)

SHELLY. *(Yelling into the living room.)* It's a Blue Spruce. Nine feet, just like you asked for!

DOTTY. *(DOTTY screams at the top of her lungs as if she is being stabbed.)* Look at it! Shelly you *did* THAT! Donnie look at what my daughter did!

(DONNIE begins to go and SHELLY stops him.)

SHELLY. Look! It's getting worse every day and before I take a bullet to her head and mine, I thought I'd cheat the clock gatdamnit!

ADAM. *(Offstage.)* Wow, that's ginormous! How did you get it in here?

DONNIE. She's not that bad. She just forgets.

SHELLY. And forgets and forgets. Wake up "Golden Boy" –

DOTTY. *(Offstage.)* Let's break out the decorations!

DONNIE. Golden Boy?

ADAM. *(Offstage.)* It's kinda late, Momma Dotty.

SHELLY. Daddy's Golden Boy. Fingers made out of gold.

DONNIE. Stop calling me that, I don't want to be called that –

SHELLY. Why? What's wrong with that? Why you so touchy?

DONNIE. Robert Frost, "Nothing Gold Can Stay."

SHELLY. Why the fuck are you quoting Robert Frost?

DOTTY. *(Offstage.)* Don't tell me you gays aren't into decorating anymore?

DONNIE. I just don't –

SHELLY. Donnie, she's getting worse every single day.

ADAM. *(Offstage.)* Oh no we still decorate. Butch, leather or flaming queen! We still decorate. Let's decorate! I'm not sleepy anyway!

DOTTY. *(Offstage.)* Neither am I! That Aurora Borealis!

ADAM. *(Offstage.)* Did you smell something on Donnie's breath, Mom?

SHELLY. What kind of money you got?

(DOTTY and ADAM re-enter.)

DONNIE. What kind of money I got? How about… HI? Good to see you little brother! Merry Fucking Christmas.

SHELLY. Ain't nobody got time for that.

DOTTY. Donnie, watch your mouth. You can express yourself better than that. We all need to learn to stop this gatdamn cussin. Come on Adam, down in the basement I've got decorations that would put Martha Stewart to shame.

SHELLY. WAIT! WAIT! HOLD UP! What y'all doing?

ADAM. Decorating the tree.

SHELLY. It's the middle of the night!

DOTTY. I'm up!

ADAM. She's up!

DOTTY. I'm up!

DONNIE. She's up!

SHELLY. She's up, I'm up, we're all fucking UP!

DOTTY. Language!

SHELLY. Go 'head, go 'head!

DOTTY. I wasn't asking you Shelly! What's wrong with you Donnie?

DONNIE. Nothing Mom.

ADAM. Nothing is wrong with him Mom.

DOTTY. Y'all fighting? Let's deal with it!

SHELLY. Family meeting! I'll start a list.

DONNIE. No, Mom, no! Shelly!

DOTTY. Your father always called a family meeting so that we could nip // it all in the bud! Don't let things fester! Eats up a family. Nip it!

DONNIE. // Mom, Dad always wanted to nip things in the bud before people could really process what they were feeling. He outed me before I could. Telling everybody at the dinner table that I was gay. // I was sixteen. I didn't really know yet.

DOTTY. // But he was fine with it. We all were. He just called a spade a spade. And you ARE gay.

SHELLY. You are Donnie! You *really* are.

DOTTY. Give him a kiss.

DONNIE. No!

DOTTY. Give my Adam a kiss!

DONNIE. No!

>   (**DOTTY** *grabs* **DONNIE** *as he stands.*)

DOTTY. Adam, get him!

>   (**ADAM** *kisses* **DONNIE**. *More like tastes his lips. It is not a romantic kiss. It is purely informational.*)

ADAM. Chicken, two oatmeal cookies, and lemonade!

>   (**DOTTY** *and* **ADAM** *high five!*)

DONNIE. No! Chicken! THREE oatmeal cookies and lemonade!

ADAM. The fast is over. Donnie! FUCK!

SHELLY. Language.

DONNIE. I'm sorry.

ADAM. *(To* **DOTTY***.)* I'm sorry.

DONNIE. No, I'm really sorry.

ADAM. That was expensive, Donnie.

DONNIE. We shouldn't have scheduled it right before the holidays.

ADAM. I can't believe you couldn't hold out a few more days.

DONNIE. IT'S CHRISTMAS! I'm hungry.

DOTTY. You have always been hungry.

ADAM. It's okay.

DONNIE. I'm sorry. We'll do it again after New Year's.

ADAM. No worries. I knew you couldn't stick it out.

DONNIE. Oh really. You got to give some to get some.

SHELLY. What's that supposed to mean?

ADAM. Come on Mom! The DECORATIONS!

>   (**ADAM** *and* **DOTTY** *exit into the living room.*)

SHELLY. Okay, we'll put a pin in that conversation. I need your help Donnie. We gotta deal with Mom's condition.

DONNIE. Can we please talk about this in the morning, when we can all think straight? We can get Averie over here in the morning. It's late.

SHELLY. OK. Fine.

(*Silence.*)

Whatchu doing up anyway?

DONNIE. I'M FUCKING STARVING!

SHELLY. OK. Unhinged.

(*Offstage laughter from* **DOTTY** *and* **ADAM**.)

DONNIE. Adam and I have been on a juice cleanse.

SHELLY. Why the fuck you doing that?

DONNIE. To CLEANSE! RESET! DETOX!

SHELLY. You doin' drugs or something?

DONNIE. No, no, no, I'm trying to get more healthy. You know, like you are supposed to, when you –

SHELLY. Are a woman of a certain age? Well we need to get very healthy in the way that we deal with Mom's reality! In the morning we will talk about how everybody, meaning you and Averie, are going to have to figure out a way to cough up some money.

DONNIE. I told you last month that my money is funny and my change is strange.

SHELLY. Well then you have to make some hard financial choices.

DONNIE. I'm chasing money. I'm a writer!

SHELLY. Even I know that THAT is not a lucrative career!

DONNIE. PAUSE!

SHELLY. You are so smart.

DONNIE. PAUSE!

SHELLY. You got into Wharton.

DONNIE. Let's not beat that dead horse.

SHELLY. You have the brains to do something that ACTUALLY turns an income.

DONNIE. I turn an income – it's just more precarious than one would hope.

SHELLY. I still don't understand how you can make money being a...what do you call what you do?

DONNIE. I'm a musicologist Shelly.

SHELLY. Someone who loves music and gets paid for it. I don't understand.

DONNIE. I love music! I am an archivist.

SHELLY. And...

DONNIE. I am freelancing right now, there are no staff positions for music critics.

SHELLY. Why?

DONNIE. I don't know! I am a dying breed! Print media is under attack from the ravages of social media and any dimwit who can create a blog and bolster his uninformed opinions // to his list of followers and spread it like a –

SHELLY. // This sounds a little too political for this time of night. *(Beat.)* This is what I get for opening up Pandora's Box. Go ahead baby brother. Unleash! *(Beat.)* I have nothing else going on in my life. *(Beat.)* Give me your tired, your poor, your huddled masses yearning to breathe free, the wretched refuse of your teeming shore.

DONNIE. // THAT'S THE WHOLE POINT! I am trying to salvage our cultural history by being an archivist of our music. If we don't record our history we are doomed. It is not only only in our baselines and song stylings but it is in the swagger in our walk. The rhythm of our talk. We need the griots of our time so that we know who we are. Raise up the youth and let them walk tall, pants up and eyes forward! No more *(Sounding like the lyrics of the* Good Times *anthem.)* Shuckin and-a-ST-R-IVIN'!

   (Silence.)

SHELLY. So you don't have any money?

DONNIE. No, not right now. I am doing some freelance work.

(Offstage laughter from **DOTTY** *and* **ADAM**.*)*

SHELLY. Maybe you can get a steady job at like Costco or something!

DONNIE. *(Squeals.)* WHAT?!

SHELLY. I've been looking at brochures and there are some good care facilities not too far. I don't want to put her in some bootleg one where she will die in a year because they ain't monitoring her heart or something.

DONNIE. What's wrong with her heart?

SHELLY. She's got a heart condition.

DONNIE. WHAT?

SHELLY. You act like I've never told you.

DONNIE. *(Squealing.)* YOU NEVER TOLD ME!

SHELLY. Yes I did. I told you. Shhh, quiet!

DONNIE. No, you quiet! I would remember you telling me that Mom had a heart condition!

SHELLY. Okay, well, she does! It's manageable so it's not something to really worry about. It's not really a heart condition, per se, she just has to watch her cholesterol. Get heart happy. Back up off, the soul food.

DONNIE. Well that's much different than a heart condition!

SHELLY. I'M OVERWHELMED! Okay?

DONNIE. MUCH!

SHELLY. I AM EXHAUSTED! You and Adam can move down here and help out until we –

DONNIE. Unh-uh! That is not possible!

SHELLY. You ain't got a steady job, so why not?

DONNIE. You've got to be kidding. I create for a living.

SHELLY. Well, sort of.

DONNIE. I. Have. A. Life. In. New. York. It. Is. Not. Possible!

SHELLY. I. Don't. Have. A. Life. Here. In. Phila. Del. Phia! We gonna have to MAKE it possible. Somehow! Well at least until… Mom's gonna kill herself.

DONNIE. *(Shrieks.)* WHAT?!

SHELLY. I know, I know, it's HORRIBLE, but she's planning it. I think that's what she is plotting with Fidel.

DONNIE. WHAT? What are you saying?

SHELLY. Am I speaking Chinese? They are plotting!

DONNIE. Shelly, what the fuck are you talking about?

SHELLY. Sshh, ssshh. She said that she didn't want to be a burden and she was going to go when she was ready.

DONNIE. That doesn't mean that she is going to kill herself! She's not that bad. She's in the early stage.

SHELLY. The early stage has passed little brother. You see it. You can't deny it anymore. We are in the middle. I've watched it, with my own two eyes. I live in this city and I am over here most of the time! Her disease is crashing all around us. I'm sorry I couldn't fit that into a TEXT!

DONNIE. IT'S THE 21ST CENTURY! I TEXT! WE ALL TEXT!

SHELLY. Not me. Not about stuff like this.

DONNIE. I'M HUNGRY!

SHELLY. Boy, eat something!

> *(Offstage laughter from* **DOTTY** *and* **ADAM**. **DONNIE** *opens the fridge and pulls out the chicken and starts eating. He sits.)*

I'm sorry to be so... HARSH. Donnie, brother, she is slipping fast and her plan for killing herself might be a thought that will pass. *(She snaps her fingers.)* Like this! So, the obvious plan would be to get her into a care facility.

DONNIE. She won't go for that! We can't put her into a home. We can't.

SHELLY. It's not a home. It's care.

DONNIE. She won't go for that.

SHELLY. She will have to. She is no longer the mother that we once had that is so fully in control of everything. She forgets to eat, to take her meds, where the bathroom is —

DONNIE. Okay! OKAY! Please STOP! You are like a battering ram. Just…

> *(Silence.)*

I just need a minute.

> *(Silence.)*

SHELLY. Okay.

> *(Silence.)*

You alright?

DONNIE. You talk to Averie?

SHELLY. We're not speaking.

DONNIE. She lives with you!

SHELLY. I let her stay in my basement. That is about as sisterly as I can get with a woman who refuses to get her life together.

DONNIE. *(Under his breath.)* Like you are any better.

SHELLY. What?

DONNIE. I didn't say anything.

SHELLY. We just stay out of each other's way. She's good with Jason, I will give her that. She is entertaining to him.

DONNIE. You two need to cut it out. You're just alike, that's the problem.

SHELLY. *(Terse.)* I am nothing like your sister!

> *(Silence.)*

DONNIE. Okay, whatever.

> *(Silence. Offstage laughter from* **DOTTY** *and* **ADAM**. *A record comes on. "UNCHAIN MY HEART" by Ray Charles, followed by "QUE SERA SERA" by*

Doris Day, etc.* as the scene continues. Every so often we hear interstitial sound from **ADAM** *and* **DOTTY***, such as "Oh, I love this song!" etc.* **DOTTY** *can sing along and so can* **ADAM** *every so often. We know that there is life in the other room.)*

SHELLY. Are they playing music?

*(***SHELLY*** begins to head toward the living room.)*

DONNIE. Leave it. Leave it.

*(***SHELLY*** begins to pour tea.)*

(Silence.)

So you got a tree for Mom?

SHELLY. Yeah, a big ass tree, Jackie helped me drag it in here.

DONNIE. What?

SHELLY. She's back. Came by earlier to borrow sheets.

DONNIE. She has finally emerged. Texting me that she couldn't make it to my wedding was the last I heard from her.

SHELLY. She's on the run.

DONNIE. From what?

SHELLY. She's pregnant.

DONNIE. Girl, who?

SHELLY. Jackie.

DONNIE. Really? With who?

SHELLY. Some married dude. Don't tell her I told you.

DONNIE. Some married dude? What is she doing with some married dude?

SHELLY. She was his side piece.

*A license to produce *Dot* does not include a performance license for "Unchain My Heart" or "Que Sera Sera." Please see Music Use Note on page 3 for further information.

DONNIE. What? That is not like her. She is such a traditionalist. She always dreamed of the husband, two kids and driving a family van.

SHELLY. No she dreamed of YOU, the two kids and driving a family van.

DONNIE. That was twenty years ago.

SHELLY. She's not over it.

DONNIE. What?

SHELLY. Sometimes it's not easy for women to move past trauma. It shows up one way or another. I know, I'm a woman! And just by being a woman, I'm in trauma!

DONNIE. No, you choose to be in trauma.

SHELLY. No, YOU choose to be in trauma.

DONNIE. I'm a black man in America. I OWN trauma.

    (Silence.)

SHELLY. You win.

DONNIE. Is she gonna keep it?

SHELLY. Is she gonna keep it? She's forty! Forty ain't no time to be having no baby. She should be putting extra money in her IRA. She is headed for the *Guinness Book of World Records.*

DONNIE. You're an idiot. That is not too old.

SHELLY. For who? No, no, no, no too many possibilities for complications besides the fact that she is pregnant by a married man, thank you very much.

DONNIE. You are one to talk.

SHELLY. No, no, no –

DONNIE. A married man?

SHELLY. Getting some man to stick it in you without a condom and running across state lines and making sure he never knows, is what I did. He was good-looking, smart, and healthy and I was ready to be a mother. Case closed.

DONNIE. Jason is nine, does he ever ask about his dad?

SHELLY. Case closed.

DONNIE. He is nine now he needs to know something.

SHELLY. No he don't. I'm his mother and his father.

DONNIE. He must ask.

SHELLY. I squashed it last week.

DONNIE. What did you say?

SHELLY. Immaculate Conception! It worked for Mary. Jesus didn't go around Jerusalem talking about "where's my father?"

DONNIE. Because he was the son of God.

SHELLY. Case closed!

(*Silence.*)

DONNIE. So my high school sweetheart is having a baby?

SHELLY. Well…it's nice to know that somebody has been having sex. Good ole Jackie.

DONNIE. Tell me about it!

SHELLY. It's a damn shame when you can't even remember the last time you had – Wait a minute, you ain't havi –

DONNIE. No. (*Beat.*) We just started speaking a few days ago after moving around the apartment without speaking to each other after a fight about a pair of skinny jeans.

SHELLY. Gay.

DONNIE. It was stupid, I don't really want to talk about it. I'm afraid that we are growing apart and I thought we finally got married after seven years and that he would be ready to have a family. I want more than just me and him.

SHELLY. Really? I've never heard you say that. I thought gay boys were more selfish than that.

DONNIE. (*Dry.*) Fuck you Shelly.

SHELLY. (*Drier.*) Fuck you Donnie.

(**DOTTY** *enters furiously.*)

DOTTY. Shelly, where did you put the key to that trunk?

SHELLY. I don't know where that key is Mom.

DOTTY. I'm gonna need that key.

(**ADAM** *enters.*)

ADAM. Mom?

SHELLY. Mom, I don't know what you do with things.

DONNIE. Adam, what's going on?

ADAM. Mom started going though the drawer looking for keys.

DONNIE. What keys?

ADAM. I don't know.

SHELLY. Mom, I'm not giving you the car keys!

DONNIE. Shelly, don't be so short.

DOTTY. Not my car keys! The key to the trunk where I put my stuff –

SHELLY. I gave it to Fidel.

DOTTY. They are my keys Shelly! You can't give away MY keys.

DONNIE. He will be over in the morning Mom. We can get them for you then.

DOTTY. Stop hiding my things!

ADAM. Mom, did you still want to decorate the tree?

DOTTY. (*Emphatically.*) What tree?

> (*Silence.*)
>
> (*Silence.*)
>
> (*Silence.*)
>
> (*Everyone stares at one another.* **DOTTY** *tries to cover up that she knows what is going on, as she has been doing.*)

OK, yeah. I want to decorate a tree.

ADAM. OK. Let's decorate the tree. There is one in the living room.

> (**ADAM** *and* **DOTTY** *exit into the living room. Suddenly we hear a scream like before of bloody murder from* **DOTTY**.)

DOTTY. OH, WOW, LOOK AT THAT!

(Silence.)

DONNIE. She's not well.

SHELLY. No, she's not.

(Silence.)

This morning before breakfast Mom told me that she is so worried that Daddy stays in bed all day and doesn't get up. She said, she kisses and hugs him and lays under his arm and he doesn't get up.

*(**DONNIE** sobers. He understands.)*

In and out, in and out, in and out. But something inside her stays right there. Right at that moment. Trauma.

DONNIE. *(Muffles his scream.)* AAAAAAHHHHHHHH HHHH!

*(**SHELLY** goes to her brother and touches his back. She opens her heart to him.)*

SHELLY. I need you. I need you and Averie to step up. Now.

(They hug.)

DONNIE. I'll try. I don't know how.

SHELLY. Neither do I. But it's something we can't avoid. Like the coming of another holiday or Averie's coming in the morning!

*(**AVERIE** bursts in from the back door!)*

AVERIE. HEY DONNIE!

DONNIE. // Oh my God! SHIT!

SHELLY. // What the! Girl, you can't be busting in doors at this hour!

AVERIE. *(Bear hugs **DONNIE**.)* DONNIE! HEY BROTHER! MERRY CHRISTMAS!

DONNIE. You scared the shit out of me.

AVERIE. BOY STOP BEING SO SCARY!

SHELLY. WHAT ARE YOU DOING HERE AT THIS TIME OF NIGHT?

AVERIE. HI SHELLY! OH, ARE YOU SPEAKING TO ME? HI SHELLY!

SHELLY. *(To* **DONNIE.***)* I'm going to bed. We will discuss MUCH in the morning.

AVERIE. I thought you would be at your house tonight so I came to stay with Mommy!

SHELLY. No I'm here.

AVERIE. YOU ARE SPEAKING TO ME! HI SIS! MERRY CHRISTMAS *(She embraces* **SHELLY.***)* OH, YOU RED NOW?

SHELLY. Goodnight!

DOTTY. *(Offstage.)* DONNIE, SHELLY, COME DECORATE THE TREE!

AVERIE. MOMMY, WHATCHU DOING UP?

DOTTY. *(Offstage.)* WHO'S THAT?

AVERIE. IT'S YOUR BABY GIRL!

DOTTY. *(Offstage.)* AVERIE COME ON IN HERE! *(We begin to hear "SLEIGH RIDE" by Lee Anderson.*)*

AVERIE. *(She sees the tree, and screams at the top of her lungs, as if she is getting murdered.)* THAT TREE IS HUGE! HEY ADAM! WE GONNA DECORATE THE FUCK OUT OF IT! OOO I'M SORRY MOMMY I SAID FUCK! COME ON Y'ALL WE ABOUT TO HAVE A MERRY FUCKING CHRISTMAS!

> *(Blackout.)*

End of Act One

---

* A license to produce *Dot* does not include a performance license for "Sleigh Ride." Please see Music Use Note on page 3 for further information.

TURN IT ALL OVER

(We hear the sounds of Nat King Cole's "THE HAPPIEST CHRISTMAS TREE."* It is playing on the record player. The next morning. Living room. Tasteful and well lived-in. There is a baby grand piano with photos of family members adorning it. It is well-preserved and polished. There is a proper living room set of furniture including a sofa, coffee and side tables. It is a house that has raised many children. The nine-foot tall Blue Spruce is decorated to perfection. There is a desk with a computer on it. **DOTTY** *is on the couch going through a shallow box.* **FIDEL***, a good-looking Central Asian guy, twenty-eight years old, is stringing Christmas lights around the window. It is nine a.m.* **DOTTY** *is wide awake. She is obsessive about organizing her thoughts this morning. She is not reveling in memory, she is organizing her thoughts.)*

DOTTY. Fidel, don't string the colored ones up there. String up the white ones. Save the coloreds for the front yard! I want the colored ones to stop traffic! *(Back to the box.)*

FIDEL. What are you doing, Mrs. Dotty?

DOTTY. I have been trying to get these pictures organized for years, for my grandson Jason. You know how you just toss the envelopes from the Foto Mat in the drawer and they just stack up for years?

FIDEL. No, I don't think so.

---

* A license to produce *Dot* does not include a performance license for "The Happiest Christmas Tree." Please see Music Use Note on page 3 for further information.

DOTTY. Wait a minute, they don't have Foto Mats anymore! They sure probably never had 'em back in um, in um…

FIDEL. Kazakhstan? I'm not sure. I don't think so.

DOTTY. Where did they all go?

FIDEL. I don't know.

DOTTY. Like aliens just came down and swooped them all up. *(Shows* **FIDEL**.*)* They had a little place for negatives. Donnie used to love to look at the negatives. Said that the world looked so different in the negatives, kind of mystical. Donnie. My middle child. He is forty years old. Play that song you like. We need some music in this house. Wake 'em up.

> (**FIDEL** *smiles. And runs to the record player. He plays Barbra Streisand's "SO MANY STARS."*)

Look at this. You know what this is?

> (**FIDEL** *looks at the photograph and shakes his head no.*)

That, there, is the Royal Pavilion. It's in Brighton, England. Made for this King. George. The third? Fourth? Third. No Fourth! Fourth! That's right the fourth! George the fourth. Wait!

> (**DOTTY** *reaches for a recorder and hits record.*)

Jason-George the fourth. He was the prince of Wales. He was fascinated with the Orient. Can I say that now? Is that P.C.?

FIDEL. P.C.?

DOTTY. Orient. Well that's what it was called. The Orient.

> (**AVERIE** *comes down the stairs, fully dressed. Looking as fabulous as ever.*)

AVERIE. Mommy, I'll be right back. I gotta go pick up a little sumptin' sumptin' from my job. I would have

---

* A license to produce *Dot* does not include a performance license for "So Many Stars." Please see Music Use Note on page 3 for further information.

brought it with me last night but our discount comes through on Christmas Eve, you know what I'm sayin'?

(AVERIE *takes the keys from their hiding place in the Liberty Bell on the piano.*)

DOTTY. OK.

(DOTTY *stares at the picture, now a bit confused.*)

AVERIE. What's yo name again?

FIDEL. Fidel.

(AVERIE *pulls some cash from her bra.*)

AVERIE. Fidel, look, I know my sister is paying you, but here is a little extra for the holidays.

FIDEL. No, no. I can't.

AVERIE. Oh yes you can and you will. Between you and me. You taking good care of my mommy. Alright boo?

FIDEL. Okay. Thank you Ms. Averie.

AVERIE. *(Flirty.)* Don't be calling me Ms. Averie with that sweet little glint in your eye. You playing with fire.

FIDEL. "You go girl!"

AVERIE. Mommy I'll be right back! You alright?

DOTTY. I'm fine. I'm fine.

AVERIE. Looking at those old memories hunh?

(AVERIE *gives* FIDEL *a wink and gestures to keep an eye on* DOTTY, *and exits. Silence.* DOTTY *stares at* FIDEL.)

FIDEL. Royal Pavilion. *(Beat.)* You were telling me about the Royal Pavilion. *(Beat.)* Tell me about the Royal Pavilion in Brighton, England. Who took you there?

DOTTY. Richard. Richard my husband.

FIDEL. Really?

DOTTY. Nobody was going to places like London around here in the 1960s. Richard is...was a ear, nose and throat doctor. Went to Howard University. Then on to the University of Pennsylvania. That's where we met. The University of Pennsylvania. I was working at

the University, in the cafeteria, as a cashier. Richard
came to my line everyday for two months before I said
to him, point blank, "When you gonna take me to a
picture show and buy a girl a drink?"

    (**FIDEL** *laughs.*)

We were married a year later and Richard showed me
that Royal Pavilion slapped down in the middle of town.
Domes and towers. Who sings this?

FIDEL. Bar-bar-a.

DOTTY. Barbara?

    (**DOTTY** *has lost her thought.* **FIDEL** *looks
    confused. Then he picks up on this story.*)

FIDEL. Remember? Domes and towers.

DOTTY. What's that honey?

    (**FIDEL** *turns off the record player.*)

FIDEL. Domes and towers. The Pavilion. Husband.

DOTTY. My husband?

    (**DOTTY** *stares intently.* **FIDEL** *does his best girly
    girl impression.*)

FIDEL. Buy a girl a drink?

    (**DOTTY** *smiles.*)

    Orient.

    (*The alarm on* **FIDEL**'*s phone goes off.*)

DOTTY. Oh that thing scares me!

FIDEL. Sorry. (*He goes into the kitchen.*)

DOTTY. You gotta get a better ring for that thing.

FIDEL. Sorry. (*From offstage*)

DOTTY. What am I looking for?

    (**FIDEL** *returns.*)

FIDEL. Medicine.

DOTTY. (*Frustrated with herself.*) What am I looking for?

FIDEL. Medicine.

DOTTY. *(Quietly frustrated.)* What, what, what?

FIDEL. I get Ms. Shelly for you?

DOTTY. No! No. Sit. Sit with me. *(They sit quietly for a long moment.)* Can I tell you something?

(**FIDEL** *nods and waits.*)

Do you know what cognitive...cognitive... I keep forgetting the last word of it, is? It's like decline or something. It's got worse. I forget things I just said or did. I cannot pick up my clothes. Get organized. I lose everything. I forget appointments even after I write them down. And the worst thing is that I can't remember people's names, the way they look to me and more and more I am having trouble finding the right words to say.

(**DOTTY** *thinks.*)

FIDEL. You can say it.

(Silence.)

DOTTY. *(Simply.)* I'm scared.

FIDEL. Okay.

(Silence.)

Okay. You said it. It's okay.

(Silence.)

DOTTY. Thank you.

(Silence.)

Do you understand me?

FIDEL. Yes.

DOTTY. Do you understand...us?

(**FIDEL** *thinks.*)

FIDEL. Sometimes...no.

DOTTY. You get confused?

FIDEL. Yes. Sometimes. The rules of English language don't make sense.

DOTTY. To me either. *(Then.)* I'm getting confused all the time.

> (**FIDEL** *sits next to* **DOTTY**. *She looks intently at* **FIDEL**. *He holds* **DOTTY**'s *hand. Silence. Silence Silence.*)

FIDEL. You okay?

> (**DOTTY** *stares into nothingness.*)

Medicine?

DOTTY. You got the cutest little accent. What is medicine in Russian?

FIDEL. Leekarstva.

DOTTY. Lik-ars-vka.

FIDEL. Leekarstva.

DOTTY. Leek-harv-sta.

FIDEL. Medicine.

DOTTY. Medicine. I guess that is my Russian word of the day. *(Laughs.)* Doesn't that make your brain hurt?

> (**FIDEL** *and* **DOTTY** *share a little laugh.*)

> (**DOTTY** *gets close to* **FIDEL** *and whispers.*)

Fidel, remember to gather those gifts up for me and help me to set it up for Christmas. You are going to help me right?

FIDEL. Right. Gotcha!

DOTTY. I got you squared away. I scratch your back –

FIDEL. And I scratch mine.

DOTTY. We gotta stick together. You and me.

FIDEL. Yes. Yes. One Donepezil.

DOTTY. One Donepezil. Bottoms up!

> (**DOTTY** *begins to down the pill. The front door bursts opens and it is* **JACKIE**. **DOTTY** *chokes or spits the pill out.*)

JACKIE. Mrs. Shealy!

DOTTY. Shit! What the hell? Scared me half to death!

JACKIE. Oh, I am so sorry!

DOTTY. You can't just be busting through doors around here!

JACKIE. I'm sorry! I was just returning the linen that I borrowed.

DOTTY. If I still had my .32 I would have blown your head off.

JACKIE. I wasn't thinking. I'll just leave them here and go.

DOTTY. You can't be sneaking in doors! This is the hood! THE HOOD!

JACKIE. I am so sorry. I'm going back to New York.

DOTTY. Wait a minute, wait a minute. Fidel I think I need another round. I can't eat this pill from up off of the floor.

> (FIDEL *looks confused.*)

More Leeky.

> (FIDEL *looks even more confused.*)

Leeksharvis. Medicine. More sweetie.

> (FIDEL *understands and runs into the kitchen.*)

JACKIE. I am so sorry.

DOTTY. It's alright. I was just in the middle of my Russian word of the day.

JACKIE. What was it?

DOTTY. Honey, I wish I knew.

JACKIE. Mrs. Shealy, Dotty, Mrs. Shealy I'm going back to New York I have this Zipcar out there and they are kind but notorious and it is sure as shinola costing me a fortune in late fees and I have to make some decisions and those will require me to actually deal with what I have going on in New York and I temporarily lost my mind I didn't even bring any make-up or underwear –

DOTTY. Sit down. You're confusing me.

JACKIE. I really should go.

DOTTY. Whose baby is it?

JACKIE. You know. Shelly told you?

DOTTY. I just know. Women know other women. I've known you all of your life.

JACKIE. *(She sits.)* Some asshole. Bad choice. Baaaaaad choice.

DOTTY. *(Simply.)* He's a dick.

JACKIE. He's a dick. I gotta go back to New York and face my truth.

>   (FIDEL *enters with the medicine.*)

DOTTY. I'm starting to face mine.

JACKIE. I'm sorry Mrs. Shealy. I didn't know.

FIDEL. One Donepezil.

DOTTY. One Donepezil. Bottoms up.

>   (DOTTY *downs the Donepezil and drinks the full
>   glass of water.*)

It slows down the progression.

(Earnestly.) It's Alzheimer's. I should have told you. I probably forgot. *(She laughs.)*

JACKIE. That's not funny.

DOTTY. It's hilarious. *(She sobers.)* My doctor said it is better to come from me. To have no shame. No shame about it.

JACKIE. *(She cries.)* Oh, Mrs. Shealy, I am so sorry.

DOTTY. This is EXACTLY why I don't tell people. What am I supposed to do with this?

JACKIE. I'm sorry.

DOTTY. It's alright, it's alright. Stop all this. It's Christmas Eve. I'm not dead.

JACKIE. Shelly says that you want to kill yourself.

>   *(Silence.)*

Is that true?

>   *(Silence.)*

DOTTY. I wanted to die. When I found out, I wanted to die.

(Silence.)

I know what's happening. And if I had the choice of fading away or just going away, which one do you think I'd choose?

(Silence.)

(Silence.)

(Silence.)

JACKIE. Is there anything I can do. Anything you need?

(Silence.)

DOTTY. I need...my mind.

(Silence.)

JACKIE. Life is just not turning out the way we hoped it would, right?

DOTTY. Nothing does. That is the fucked up secret of life.

JACKIE. Don't you feel mad? I mean what the fuck? Alzheimer's?

DOTTY. I do. I'm mad one minute, sad the next.

JACKIE. Me too. I just want some peace, you know.

DOTTY. Me too. It gets so noisy in here. *(Points to her head.)*

JACKIE. Me too. *(Beat.)* I love you Mrs. Shealy. I'll be back soon. I should go now before everyone wakes up.

DOTTY. You can't leave without saying Merry Christmas.

JACKIE. But –

DOTTY. Donnie and Adam are here. Adam. His husband.

JACKIE. I know. I met him the last time I was here. Actually, walked in on them kissing and hugged up on the couch.

DOTTY. That bothered you?

JACKIE. No, no, that didn't bother me. It's just...we used to kiss on that couch.

DOTTY. You know, I always knew he was gay? Even as you two were running around here after each other like Heckle and Jeckle. I always knew. A mother ALWAYS knows. Even if she tries to look the other way, like Marquis' mother, Lena, down the block. That boy wears more make-up than I do and she still tells me how all the women are always after him at church. Hmph – after him to see what kind of foundation he is wearing! *(She laughs and hoots.)*

(JACKIE looks at the photos in DOTTY's box.)

Look at that! Your parents. Me and my husband. Sharp! When people drive through this neighborhood, all they see are run down houses and the ravages of an economic depression. No one is even aware of the history here.

JACKIE. I am. I'm proud of where I come from. It may look a little different but I can feel it is all still right here. You're all still here.

(Silence.)

DOTTY. I'm not so sure. I tell you what, I'm gonna record as much as I can hold on to.

FIDEL. *(In very broken English.)* Can I call home?

DOTTY. What's that?

FIDEL. Home. Phone home.

DOTTY. Sure E.T.

(FIDEL goes over to the computer and speaks softly under this.)

E.T. phone home. *(Laughs.)* That was some movie. He was so cute. I wonder what ever happened to him. E.T. What did that stand for?

JACKIE. Extra-Terrestrial.

DOTTY. Extra-Terrestrial. E.T. Ain't that something. If E.T. came out now in the cineplex, would he text home? Nawwww. E.T. knows. It's not the same as the sound of a warm voice. Calling you home.

(She reaches out her finger to JACKIE and JACKIE does the same.)

Reaching out that finger hoping that someone is reaching out that little finger to you. *(Very E.T.)* Phone home.

(Silence.)

Did you find my keys?

JACKIE. What keys?

DOTTY. The keys to that trunk in the basement.

JACKIE. I don't know anything about keys, Mrs. Shealy.

DOTTY. Mrs. Shealy? Oh we are awfully proper today aren't we Mrs. Shealy. You always been uppity after we sent you to those private schools. I told Richard not to put y'all in those damned schools. I went to public school and look at me.

JACKIE. Unh-hunh.

DOTTY. Jack and Jill socials. Trying to turn you and your sister into Grace Kelly or something.

JACKIE. Mrs. Shealy, It's me Jackie. Jackie.

DOTTY. I know Jackie. Jackie I know who the hell you are!

JACKIE. Mrs. Shealy! *(She yells.)* Shelly!

> **(FIDEL** *takes off headphones and looks up from Skype on the computer.)*

FIDEL. Everything okay? –

JACKIE. I think we need Shelly –

DOTTY. No, I'm –

JACKIE. Mrs. Shealy needs a glass of water –

> **(FIDEL** *runs off and grabs a glass of water from the kitchen.)*

DOTTY. MRS. SHEALY NEEDS NOTHING. Stop treating me like a child! I am your mother.

JACKIE. Mrs. Shealy please. I don't mean to upset you. It's me Jackie. Jackie.

DOTTY. Damnit, // damnit, damnit, damn.

JACKIE. I didn't mean to upset you – **(DOTTY** *stares at* **JACKIE**.*)*

(Silence.)

(Silence.)

(Silence.)

DOTTY. I'm sorry.

JACKIE. No, no, it's fine, it's fine.

(FIDEL returns with the glass of water.)

DOTTY. Thank you Fidel. Tell your momma I said hi. Hi momma.

FIDEL. *(In Russian.)* Она сказала привет мамочка *[Translation: Mrs. Shealy says hi, Momma.]*

JACKIE. It's fine.

DOTTY. No. It's not. I am losing, Jackie.

JACKIE. Mrs. Shealy, have you expressed this to your children?

DOTTY. They know it but they don't know how to deal with it. They are my children. They only see me as a mother and not as a woman. *(Beat.)* What time is it?

JACKIE. It's nine-twenty in the morning.

DOTTY. What day?

JACKIE. Christmas Eve.

DOTTY. Nine-twenty in the morning on Christmas Eve. I just needed to make sure. Christmas Eve dinner is at five. Five. You coming?

JACKIE. No, I'm –

DOTTY. Bring your mom. There is a place for you all at the table.

JACKIE. My mom? Um…we can't.

DOTTY. But y'all come every year. Y'all come here at five. Tell your momma to bring her lemon pound cake. I'm gonna make my 7Up cake.

JACKIE. OK. OK. I will. I will be here at five.

DOTTY. What a nice family. This community is wonderful.

JACKIE. Okay.

DOTTY. See you at five?

JACKIE. See you at five.

> (JACKIE *exits.*)

FIDEL. // Бесплатно. Я собираюсь получить мое убежище и, когда это будет сделано, я буду в состоянии вернуться домой, чтобы увидеть тебя. Следующего Рождества. Не плачь, мама. Я должен идти. Я на работе. Я позвоню тебе позже. Bye Bye.

> *[Translation: For free. I'm gonna get my asylum and when that is done I will be able to come home to see you. Next Christmas. Don't cry Momma. I gotta go. I'm at work. I will call you later. Bye Bye.]*

> (**FIDEL** *is trying to hold back tears.*)

DOTTY. Fidel. You alright?

> (**SHELLY** *comes down the stairs. And the pace picks up again, messy and noisy.*)

SHELLY. FIDEL DID YOU GIVE HER, HER PILLS? MEDICINE?

> (**DONNIE** *and* **ADAM** *come down the stairs.*)

FIDEL. Yes. *(He exits into the kitchen.)*

SHELLY. Mom, why you got all these pictures out?

DONNIE. Morning.

SHELLY. Morning.

ADAM. Morning Mom, Shelly.

DOTTY. Morning.

DONNIE. Morning Mom. Are you looking for something?

SHELLY. Why is the tape recorder on?

DOTTY. I was looking through these photos. *(Calls offstage.)* Right Fidel?

DONNIE. The negatives.

SHELLY. You are so strange. You look at the pictures, fool, not the negatives.

DOTTY. *(Speaking into the recorder.)* Places, things, relatives. Cousin Cypherdean.

ADAM. Cypherdean?

SHELLY. I haven't had breakfast yet. Don't bring up Cypherdean. // *(Yells.)* Fidel! Coffee!

DOTTY. // Cypherdean was a mess. He was six-foot-four and wore a beaded gown // to Uncle David's funeral. Remember that?

DONNIE. // No one ever talked about him, he was always shrouded // in mystery.

SHELLY. // I've got my list for the market. // I've got to pick up a few things.

DOTTY. // Cypherdean walked up to the casket and fell over in it. It took me and your cousins Mudee and Sudee // to get him out of it.

ADAM. // Mudee and Sudee?

DONNIE. Nicknames for Martha and Sarah.

SHELLY. Cloves for the ham, // cinnamon sticks, eggnog, got to have eggnog, Mom.

DOTTY. // He fell OUT! He would always wait until he was the last to arrive at any family event. He always wanted all eyes on him.

DONNIE & SHELLY. That's your cousin Geoffrey but he calls himself Cypherdean.

SHELLY. Mom, do you want anything special from the market? //

DOTTY. I didn't know if you were asking me anything. You've been telling me.

SHELLY. What?

ADAM. // Cypher means zero. It also means a person or thing of no importance. A non-entity.

DONNIE. He called himself a non-entity.

ADAM. It also means a coded message. // He was a coded message.

SHELLY. // Cranberries, oranges, mini marshmallows.

DOTTY. // A coded message with tears and more drama than an episode of *Knots Landing*. *(She reveals a photo.)* Here he, um, she is.

*(**FIDEL** enters with coffee service for all.)*

ADAM. Oh my.

DONNIE. For a non-entity, she made one helluva statement! A PIONEER!

ADAM. OH HERE WE GO!

SHELLY. He wasn't settling the west! Where's my keys?

DONNIE. NO, he was settling his historically conservative black neighborhood of the East, // that was still reeling from the shock of the 1960s.

ADAM. // Oh my God! EVERYTHING IS NOT POLITICAL!

DOTTY. THE SIXTIES CHANGED EVERYTHING!

DONNIE. The non-entities paved the way for us.

ADAM. I know, I know. I'M ON YOUR SIDE.

SHELLY. HEY! HEY! CUT IT OUT!

ADAM. WE CAN BE OUR OWN CREATION!

DONNIE. THAT'S FROM *LA CAGE!*

ADAM. I KNOW IT'S FROM *LA CAGE!* If you scratch the surface everyone is just trying to find themselves. Especially at our age! Creating and recreating. I think that's healthy!

DONNIE. I DON'T BUY IT! ESPECIALLY WITH A LINE FROM A MUSICAL. PEOPLE BREAKING INTO DANCE FOR NO REASON.

ADAM. IT HAPPENS AND SOMETIMES THERE IS A GOOD REASON!

SHELLY. HEY, HEY! I'M TRYING TO DRINK MY COFFEE! THIS IS THE ONLY MOMENT OF SANITY IN ANYONE'S DAY! COFFEE!

ADAM. Sorry Shelly.

DONNIE. Sorry.

> *(Silence. They sip coffee. **DOTTY** stares at a photo from her past. It is a photo of her and her husband.)*

ADAM. We haven't met, hi! *(He now speaks a little loud, as if **FIDEL** is deaf.)* I'm Adam and you must be Fidel. This is

Donnie my husband and he is Mrs. Shealy's son. It is really nice to meet you! Merry Christmas Eve morning!

(Silence.)

(**FIDEL** *blankly stares, wondering why this man is yelling at him and is overtly friendly.*)

FIDEL. Merry Christmas Eve morning.

ADAM. He's doesn't speak English, right?

DONNIE. He speaks English, right, Shelly?

SHELLY. COFFEE!

(**FIDEL** *exits.*)

DOTTY. *(Wistful. To herself.)* Look at this picture of Richard and me.

ADAM. *(Trying to be extremely positive.)* Mom, shall we open gifts tonight or tomorrow in the morning?

DONNIE. Christmas morning. Tradition.

ADAM. Why don't we try something new? Open one gift tonight?

DONNIE. We don't do that!

ADAM. I'm just trying to lighten the mood!

SHELLY. Adam, we don't do that. We do it all about five o'clock in the morning. Jason will get up first, and he will barely have slept. Bug me to go downstairs because Santa Mom has come.

DONNIE. You told him about Santa?

SHELLY. He was getting too old for all that. My credit cards have my name on them not St. Nicholas.

ADAM. Point taken.

SHELLY. And then we all go down, coffee is brewing, breakfast starts being made and the wrapping paper covers the floor! Christmas at the Shealy's. You can't mess with tradition. So, I'm out. Watch Mom. Back in a few!

DOTTY. Put on that song, Richard. *(Silence.)* Richard, put on that song. That melancholic sweeping beautiful big band song. I forget the name of it.

DONNIE. Richard? Mom?

SHELLY. Mom, that's Adam.

DOTTY. Put it on honey –

SHELLY. Mom, that's Adam.

DOTTY. It's right there on the side of the record player.

ADAM. Okay.

DONNIE. Adam.

ADAM. Donnie, Shelly, please. (*Assuredly.*) It's okay.

> (**ADAM** *puts a song on.** We hear the flourishes of the intro.*)

DOTTY. Oh I love this song. Tradition.

ADAM. Tradition.

DOTTY. A dream.

ADAM. A dream.

DONNIE. (*Whispers.*) Adam please. I don't think it's healthy to play into this.

SHELLY. Mom –

ADAM. It's not hurting anybody.

DOTTY. Well, are you going to ask me to dance?

ADAM. (*Holds out his hand.*) Can I have this dance?

DOTTY. I thought you'd never ask.

> (**DOTTY** *curtsies and* **ADAM** *does an elaborate bow.* **DOTTY** *folds herself into* **ADAM**'s *arms. They begin to dance cheek to cheek.* **DONNIE** *and* **SHELLY** *watch.*)

Where have you been?

ADAM. I've been here. I'm always here.

DONNIE. Adam, what are you doing?

ADAM. Shhh.

---

*A license to produce *Dot* does not include a performance license for use of any copyrighted music. Samuel French and the author suggest that licensees use a song in the public domain or create an original composition.

DOTTY. Shhh. Our kids can be so nosy. Y'all sit down and watch your mommy and daddy dance. You can learn a lot about love just by watching us dance. The way your daddy puts his hand on the small of my waist. The way he looks me in the eye and whispers something in my ear that makes me laugh.

> (**ADAM** *thinks and then whispers something in her ear.* **DOTTY** *laughs and then lays her head on* **ADAM***'s shoulder.*)

I love this song. Take me for a turn around the room.

> (*They dance! It is dreamy and romantic.* **ADAM** *leads* **DOTTY** *around the room in this sweeping dance.* **DOTTY** *is as lithe and buoyant as she was at thirty-eight years old. Giddy and playful. This is just a moment. She then bursts into tears and holds* **ADAM** *for dear life.*)

DOTTY. (*She holds* **ADAM** *tight and begins to sob.*) I miss you so much. Me lying under your arm. You as cold as ice. I didn't know how I would make it without you. Raising these kids. I'm pretty strong but you take care of me. Give our children the best of everything. (*She looks over to her children who are now visibly moved.*) Now use your gifts. You all have gifts. Use your gifts! That's all I ever want from you! Me and your daddy. This life can be a dream my Michellene, my ballerina! Donatello, my pianist! And my Averie? Where is Averie?

DONNIE. I don't know. Is she upstairs, Shelly?

SHELLY. I don't know.

DONNIE. (*Trembling.*) She's coming Mom.

DOTTY. Averie, my First Lady of song. My mind is playing tricks on me Adam.

ADAM. I know.

> (**AVERIE** *bursts through the door, loaded down with a big red bucket of chitlins and groceries.*)

AVERIE. Hey y'all!

SHELLY & DONNIE. Ssshhhh.

AVERIE. Why y'all shushing?

DONNIE. SHHHHHH!

AVERIE. MOM! WHY ARE YOU DANCING ALL UP ON DONNIE'S MAN WITH THE BLINDS ALL OPEN?! THAT DON'T EVEN LOOK RIGHT!

SHELLY & DONNIE. AVERIE!

AVERIE. WELL SOMEBODY HAD TO SAY IT! JUST CLOSE THE BLINDS! YOU KNOW HOW THESE NEIGHBORS ARE! ALL UP IN THIS HOUSE! MERRY MERRY ERRBODY – I brought CHITLINS – I got them with my holiday discount, PA DOW! HAHA! WE GONNA HAVE A MERRY GATDAMN CHRISTMAS! *(She roars with laughter.)*

> *(We hear the sound of Lou Rawls "CHRISTMAS IS."* FIDEL takes the groceries from AVERIE. AVERIE follows FIDEL to the kitchen.)*

What's your name again?! Boy, don't forget these CHITLINS!

> *(DOTTY is taken upstairs by ADAM. SHELLY goes to run her errands. DONNIE goes to the kitchen. We jettison to later in the day.)*

---

*A license to produce *Dot* does not include a performance license for "Christmas Is." Please see Music Use Note on page 3 for further information.

SL(AVERIE)

(Lights up on the living room. You can see a bit of the dining room offstage right. The smell of chitlins is in the air. **SHELLY** *and* **DONNIE** *enter.* **AVERIE** *brings them chitlin samplers in small dishes.)*

AVERIE. Y'all can talk about chitlins all you want but you know you love 'em! Yes, they may stink up the house for a good forty-eight hours but they are a delicacy. That is all the slaves could eat. Everything that the slave masters didn't want and threw away and our people had to make something out of it to survive. Fatback, snouts, ears, neck bones, feet, and intestines, given to the slaves. You gotta take lemons and make some shit out of it. And if you don't...well... I don't know what to tell you. My new agent called me today and said that I am up for *Celebrity Mud Fight.* I know what y'all are going to say, but let me tell you, it's a good opportunity. To make some real money! *CELEBRITY MUD FIGHT!* Every week we would mud fight to stay in the house. And no there is no prize money, but it is a chance that would lead to financial opportunities. No need for the side-eye Shelly. Ask Donnie! He knows all about a brand. Writing those critiques about soul music and treating it like he is making anthropologic discoveries with socio-economic undertones and wearing those glasses and speaking so intelligently! It's branding. And I am about to get mine on! *(***FIDEL*** enters with a bowl for* **AVERIE.***)* I have taken the scraps up off the floor and made lemonade out of it. Me and...what's your name again?

FIDEL. Fidel.

AVERIE. Fidel Castro here, and I cleaned those suckers till they stopped squealing! Right Fidel?

FIDEL. Yes —

AVERIE. I taught Fidel how to soak and rinse those bad boys until they were squeaky clean. Got all that extra fat —

FIDEL. Right –

AVERIE. Undigested food –

FIDEL. Yes –

AVERIE. And bits of fecal matter off of 'em!

FIDEL. We sure did –

AVERIE. Clean 'em, boil the hell out of 'em with a little baking soda and salt. Season 'em up and what? Delicious! Lynnie Poo down the street, even goes so far as to throw them in the washing machine for the final rinse. Now that's crazy! She also makes bath soap out of pot liquor from collared greens but that's another story! We gonna have some pork chitlins, not chitterlings, for Christmas, because Momma said she missed her mamma's chiltin's and that's what she's gonna get. And no, they didn't come from no Whole Foods, Donnie, and they are not organic, Adam. We are having regular ole chitlins for Mom, and I am proud of my slave heritage.

We do what we got to do!

SHELLY. Where do you get this very odd modern day slave narrative from?

AVERIE. From LIFE! From LIVING! I may not have gone to college like the two of you but I've got LIFE and the knowledge of history.

SHELLY. That explains why you are living in my basement.

AVERIE. Oh are we gonna go there? //

(**ADAM** comes down from the stairs.)

ADAM. // She's resting.

SHELLY. // I'm just stating the facts!

DONNIE. // Thank you Adam.

AVERIE. And you ain't got no man!

ADAM. Of course.

SHELLY. // I don't want no man! And you don't need no man! You need some guidance!

DONNIE. // Hey!

AVERIE. // Why you mouthin?

SHELLY. // I'm not MOUTHIN! Whatever that means!

AVERIE. // Un hunh, Un hunh, I THOUGHT not!

DONNIE. // Don't start, you two.

AVERIE. *Static! Don't start none, won't be none!*

SHELLY. *STATIC!*

SHELLY & AVERIE. *Don't start none, won't be none!*

SHELLY, DONNIE & AVERIE. *STATIC! Don't start none, won't be none!*

DONNIE, AVERIE, SHELLY. *Static! Static! STATIC!*

> *(They all fall over laughing.)*

SHELLY. That was my jam! *(Beat.)* Now, about those chitlins. I made a turkey and a ham. So we don't need any slave food.

AVERIE. Mom asked for them.

SHELLY. When?

AVERIE. Last week she said she had a taste for her mother's chiltins. I make 'em just like Grandmom. I HOLD ON TO OUR FOOD HERITAGE! Someone has to. And… I could make the giblet stuffing from the drippings of your fancy turkey, too, thank you very much.

ADAM. I'm sorry Averie, we are not having carbs.

AVERIE. What?

DONNIE. Or gluten.

AVERIE. Say what, say what now?

ADAM. Or dairy.

AVERIE. Or anything that brings JOY! PURE UNADULTERATED JOY!

ADAM. You know modern agrarian practices –

AVERIE. Y'all about to get on my nerves! All this talk about carbs, gluten and dairy. You think those children in those Save the Children campaigns in Africa or South Central L.A. are thinking about their carb, gluten or dairy intake? UM… NO! They are just trying to EAT. Period. Food. PERIOD.

ADAM. Sugar is POISON.

DONNIE. Don't egg her on.

AVERIE. Everybody kills me these days. All this shit people won't eat. Oh I'm sorry, Mom said we can't cuss in the house. SORRY MOM! Fuck. Just eat but don't be a pig about it. Everything in moderation. Right Fidel? Fidel over here eats EVERY GATDAMNED thing. Why, cause he is from a third world country and people can't afford to have specialty diets. Right Fidel?

FIDEL. I eat meat.

AVERIE. SEE!

DONNIE. Okay fine, Averie. Just put the chitlins on the table as a slave food option.

AVERIE. Oh, I was. Mom!

*(**DOTTY** comes down the stairs.)*

DONNIE. Mom, I thought you were resting.

DOTTY. I can't rest. I've got things to do. It's Christmas Eve. What's that smell?

SHELLY. Mom, we got this. Everything is under control.

AVERIE. *(Yells.)* I cooked the chitlins!

DOTTY. Chitlins?

AVERIE. Just like Grandma used to make!

DOTTY. I haven't had chitlins in years.

SHELLY. Mom, I don't think you can even have chitlins. All that pork ain't good for your diet. Clogging up arteries –

AVERIE. They don't clog up nuthin! Not the way that I cleaned 'em. I cleaned the fuck –

ADAM. Language.

FIDEL. We sure did.

DONNIE. Mom, sit down.

DOTTY. I don't need to sit. I'm fine.

ADAM. You sure, Momma Dotty?

DOTTY. I'm sure, I'm sure. I need something to do. Is the turkey dressed?

SHELLY. Did it.

DOTTY. Well what about the yams and the collards?

SHELLY. Done and ready.

DOTTY. DAMN!

ADAM. Yes, did it, so you can just take it easy.

DOTTY. The sweet potato pies didn't get made did they?

DONNIE. You cooked them last night after you decorated the Christmas tree.

DOTTY. What Christmas tree?

> *(Silence.)*

SHELLY. Mom I know what you can do. Since we've got this under control would you mind getting Jason's gifts from down in the basement?

> *(**DOTTY** looks around at everyone. It looks like she is trying to focus intently.)*

DOTTY. It's Christmas Eve. Christmas Eve. (**DOTTY** *looks like she can't focus. She is desperate in her attempt to focus on the room. Then –.)* I got to organize that trunk for Jason – Fidel, where did I put that box?

FIDEL. I'll get the box.

> *(**FIDEL** picks up shoebox from desk, opens basement door. He and **DOTTY** go downstairs.)*

SHELLY. Shit. Okay. Family meeting. NOW!

> *(**SHELLY** goes over to the basement door and locks it.)*

DONNIE. Now?

SHELLY. You know a better time?

AVERIE. You are locking a woman with Alzheimer's and her illegal caregiver in the basement?

SHELLY. Just for a few minutes. We all need to talk.

ADAM. Well – I'll just go upstairs and check some emails –

SHELLY. You too, Adam. You are a part of this family. And since I can't reach you both in a timely manner – we have to lock a woman with Alzheimer's and her illegal caregiver in the basement. I have a list.

> (**SHELLY** *pulls out a list and everyone moans and groans. Expletives and all.*)

AVERIE. Not the list!

DONNIE. We are not going to have time for a list Shelly.

SHELLY. A list will help us stay on track and get things done efficiently.

AVERIE. Girl, just talk! Ain't nobody got time for your list –

SHELLY. One! We need to prepare for putting Mom in an assisted living situation and that costs.

AVERIE. She is not HARDLY going to go for that! And neither will I. WE DON'T DO THAT!

SHELLY. In like five minutes, she won't know.

AVERIE. Don't matter. We ain't white people! No offense Adam.

ADAM. None taken.

AVERIE. That's what WHITE people do!

SHELLY. You got a better plan?

AVERIE. If you get down off the cross and listen to me like I told you before, we could get her signed up over at the church, for the sick and shut in // prayer ladies, that go by houses on the daily.

SHELLY. Sick and shut in prayer ladies? Some random church ladies? With no certification whatsoever to care for my mother.

AVERIE. There you go – YOUR MOTHER!

SHELLY. You know what I meant.

AVERIE. Yeah I know what you meant. Which is why you are OVERWHELMED!

SHELLY. You have no idea what you are talking about.

AVERIE. I know EXACTLY what I am talking –

SHELLY. TWO! WE ALL NEED TO START DOING BRAIN GAMES.

AVERIE. WHAT?

SHELLY. CROSSWORD PUZZLES!

DONNIE. This isn't helping.

SHELLY. GET INFORMED AND KEEP YOUR MEMORY IN CHECK!

ADAM. SHE'S RIGHT!

DONNIE. I DON'T WANT TO THINK ABOUT IT!

SHELLY. WE HAVE TO!

AVERIE. I HEAR YOU, BUT YOU ARE WORSE THAN CASTRO!

ADAM. What does Fidel have to do with this?

SHELLY. WHAT?

AVERIE. THE DICTATOR!

ADAM. Oh –

AVERIE. All you want is your way or the freeway –

SHELLY. Wrong expression and NO. I. DON'T. All I try to do –

AVERIE. If you really want a FAMILY decision, you really have to involve the FAMILY. Not just dictate and then get mad because you feel so put upon!

ADAM. Averie is right!

AVERIE. HA!

ADAM. We should SHARE in these decisions. We should ALL have the information needed to assess these family matters.

SHELLY. YOU TWO DON'T PICK UP PHONES!

DONNIE. So you get back at us by withholding information? // THAT'S FAIR?

SHELLY. // I don't withhold information!

ADAM. When you OVERWHELM yourself you do. And that's not fair.

DONNIE. You do and that's not fair! YOU DO! And it's SPITEFUL.

(*Silence.*)

SHELLY. The thing we should deal with is the fact that she is planning on killing herself.

ADAM. *(Shrieks quietly.)* What?

DONNIE. Shelly said it but I don't believe it.

ADAM. Oh my God! You ALL withheld!

AVERIE. She doesn't mean it.

SHELLY. What do you mean she doesn't mean it? Do you know what's going on in her head?

(Pounding on the door.)

AVERIE. I don't need to know. That's not the point. Just comfort her, give her what she wants, while she still knows WHO THE FUCK WE ARE!

DOTTY. *(Offstage.)* Fidel, just turn the knob. Just turn it.

FIDEL. *(Offstage.)* I'm trying.

DOTTY. *(Offstage.)* Is it locked?

ADAM. We should open the door.

DONNIE. Hold on Mom.

SHELLY. Damn. I'mma give her a pill later so we can finish this conversation.

(Pounding on the door.)

FIDEL. *(Offstage.)* Hello?

*(**SHELLY** goes to unlock the door.)*

AVERIE. Stop giving her sleeping aids so that YOU can get rest.

*(**DOTTY** enters loaded down with Christmas gifts. **FIDEL** follows.)*

DOTTY. Why was that door locked?

SHELLY. It was just…

DONNIE, SHELLY, AVERIE. STUCK!

SHELLY. Mom what you are doing with those?

DOTTY. I want to give these out now.

DONNIE. Now? Mom. We always wait until Christmas Day.

AVERIE. I can help you get those under the tree Mom.

DOTTY. I need to give these out now.

(The doorbell rings.)

SHELLY. Who's that?

AVERIE. *(She goes to answer the door.)* Christmas caroling crackheads!

DONNIE. Mom, let me help you with those.

DOTTY. I don't need help. I want you to have these.

SHELLY. MOM JUST LET US TAKE CARE OF IT!

DOTTY. I'VE GOT THIS! I'VE GOT THIS, GATDAMNIT!

> *(Door opens.)*

JACKIE. MERRY CHRISTMAS SHEALY FAMILY!

ALL. MERRY CHRISTMAS!

> *(Everyone in the house feigns a bright and joyful greeting, immediately followed by the previous disgruntled state.)*

JACKIE. What's that smell? HEY! DONNIE!

DONNIE. HEY!

AVERIE. Look what the cat dragged in! Hey gurl!

JACKIE. Merry Christmas! Hi! I brought an Entemann's! Hi!

DONNIE. Oh my God you look great!

JACKIE. Stop lying, I look terrible.

ADAM. Hi!

JACKIE. Hi. We met briefly! A couple years ago!

ADAM. We did?

DONNIE. This is my partner Adam.

ADAM. Husband.

DONNIE. Husband.

JACKIE. Adam! Hi! You two were into some heavy petting the last time.

ADAM. Hunh?

JACKIE. On the couch.

DONNIE. What are you talking about?

JACKIE. Heavy petting on the couch a couple of years ago. Thanksgiving. It was awkward.

AVERIE. I hope you ain't still carrying that flame!

ADAM. What is she talking about?

JACKIE. I would have met you but you guys were, you know? On the couch.

AVERIE. Burn it.

ADAM. I don't know what you are talking about?

DONNIE. Wait a minute. Is that why you ran out of here and never showed back up here to eat?

ADAM. *(To* **DONNIE***.)* Who is this?

DONNIE. This is the Jackie that was my high school sweetheart.

ADAM. *(High.)* Oh! *(Low.)* Ohhhh… Nice to finally, really, meet you.

JACKIE. High school sweethearts.

ADAM. I know, you missed a fabulous wedding. You broke his heart.

JACKIE. I think it was the other way around. OVER IT!

DOTTY. SIT, Jackie. We are about to open presents. It's Christmas.

SHELLY. Christmas Eve.

DOTTY. Whatever. SIT.

JACKIE. I hope I'm not imposing. Your mom asked me to join you all for dinner.

SHELLY. I've got to go pick up Jason.

DOTTY. Get him later. Fidel –

SHELLY. Mom –

DOTTY. Fidel hand out my gifts please!

ADAM. I thought we didn't open gifts on Christmas Eve?

DOTTY. This year's different.

>   *(***FIDEL*** does this very quickly and awkwardly. Everyone stands with gift boxes.)*

FIDEL. с Новым годом *(Translation: Happy New Year!)*

>   *(Everyone looks at* **FIDEL***.)*

AVERIE. What did you say?

DOTTY. Open your gifts.

AVERIE. Open the gifts!

(They all unwrap the gift boxes.)

DONNIE. Goggles?

SHELLY. Headphones?

AVERIE. Latex gloves? Tape? Pebbles? Mom what kind of freaky deaky stuff you getting into?

DOTTY. Shut up, Averie. Explain it Fidel.

FIDEL. It's a game. It's fun. Well, sort of. She wants to put your shoes in her feet.

SHELLY. What?

ADAM. You mean our feet in her shoes.

FIDEL. I guess so. Your shoe.

AVERIE. My shoe? Oh no, I ain't putting any pebbles in my Manolo Blahniks! You do it Shelly!

SHELLY. Do what?

FIDEL. Put her shoes in your feet?

SHELLY. My shoes have been in her feet. I mean her feet in my shoes. I mean –

AVERIE. And you went to college.

SHELLY. I mean, I'm not playing this game. I have things to do.

AVERIE. OVERWHELMING YOURSELF. We all have things to do!

SHELLY. Then you do it!

DOTTY. STOP IT! Donnie, will you do it for me?

FIDEL. Your shoe.

DOTTY. You are the man of this house.

ADAM. Donnie, take off your shoe. I think I heard about this before. *(**FIDEL** puts pebbles into **DONNIE**'s shoe.)*

JACKIE. I think I did, too.

AVERIE. WHY ARE THE WHITE PEOPLE SO WELL INFORMED?

SHELLY. Spoken by the YouTube sensation.

AVERIE. But YAAAAS, I AM A SENSATION.

DOTTY. Shut up Averie! Put all this on Son? *(FIDEL puts latex gloves on DONNIE.)* Play the game for me? You will understand.

DONNIE. Okay Mom.

DOTTY. Fidel will take you through it.

AVERIE. What's supposed to happen Fidel?

DOTTY. Read those instructions for me Fidel.

> *(FIDEL takes the tape. He tapes together two fingers on each hand of DONNIE's.)*

FIDEL. And the headphones.

DONNIE. What am I doing?

AVERIE. Can he read?

DOTTY. Yes he can read. He's foreign, not stupid.

SHELLY. I barely hear the boy speak.

DOTTY. He can read. He's just shy.

FIDEL. Most people think because I am foreign, I am dumb. I'm not. I can hear too, I just don't understand your accents sometimes enough to respond.

AVERIE. He told us.

ADAM. Go on Fidel.

FIDEL. *(Reads.)* This is twelve minutes that will change your life!

AVERIE. Twelve minutes?

SHELLY. I've gotta pick up Jason!

AVERIE. That's all?

DONNIE. Food's gonna get cold Mom!

AVERIE. I would have asked for that a long time ago!

DOTTY. WILL EVERYBODY PLEASE SHUT THE FUCK UP AND LISTEN TO FIDEL?!

> *(A beat.)*

AVERIE. *(Sotto voce.)* Language.

FIDEL. *(Reads.)* Wear obstructed goggles, which help to simulate glaucoma –

AVERIE. GLAUCOMA?

FIDEL. // Cataracts or a blur in vision that is very common in later years. Latex gloves –

AVERIE. THE ONLY GAMES TO BE PLAYED OUTSIDE OF A HOSPITAL WITH LATEX GLOVES ARE –?

SHELLY. // I CAN'T HEAR THE BOY!

AVERIE. // THEN STOP INTERRUPTING!

FIDEL. // – And tape for fingers to make your hands feel arthritic, clumsy and hard to bend. Put a substance inside shoes to make it hard to walk –

SHELLY. What is this GAME? It doesn't sound like CHARADES!

DOTTY. // IT'S NOT!

FIDEL. // Earphones that emit an incessant gabbering –

SHELLY. JABBERING! JABBERING!

FIDEL. // Give this person five tasks and they only have twelve minutes to accomplish them!

DONNIE. *(Calmly.)* I don't understand? What is this Mom?

SHELLY. MOM? We don't have time to PLAY games!

DOTTY. Play it! Play it! PLAY IT!

FIDEL. *(Sweetly, to cut the tension for* **SHELLY**, **DONNIE**, *and* **AVERIE**.*)* It's like hide and seek. When you are a little kid. Except you're not.

AVERIE. Sounds like fun.

DONNIE. I'm all ready. I'll play your game Mom.

> (**DONNIE** *puts the headphones on and we hear a strange cacophony of sound. He takes them off quickly.*)

DOTTY. Play the game. Play the game for me.

> *(The headphones go back on.)*

FIDEL. I will assemble the game. Give the person five tasks. Simple things to do.

AVERIE. This gonna be fun! Look at him, he looks so CRAZY! GO TO THE CLOSET AND FIND A BLUE SWEATER.

SHELLY. I'm not playing this game. *(SHELLY retreats.)*

AVERIE. You are such a killjoy!

DONNIE. I can't hear you?

JACKIE. FIND A BLUE SWEATER IN THE CLOSET!

ADAM. PUT THE WRAPPING PAPER ON THE TABLE.

AVERIE. What else?

SHELLY. POUR ME A GLASS OF WINE!

AVERIE. Oh, you playin' now? How many is that?

FIDEL. THREE.

DONNIE. A TREE?

AVERIE. No THREE! Ignore that. FIND A BLUE SWEATER IN THE CLOSET, PUT THE WRAPPING PAPER ON THE TABLE, POUR DRUNK SHELLY A GLASS OF WINE... FIND THE SNOWMAN ON THE TREE AND...

DOTTY. PLAY "HAVE YOURSELF A MERRY LITTLE CHRISTMAS" ON THE PIANO.

DONNIE. WHAT?!

DOTTY. PLAY "HAVE YOURSELF –

DONNIE. I HEARD YOU... I HAVEN'T PLAYED IN YEARS.

AVERIE. YOU GOT IT?

SHELLY. Let's get this show on the road. I've got to pick up my boy and Christmas Eve dinner is going to get cold.

AVERIE. GO!

FIDEL. GO!

DONNIE. FIND A BLUE SWEATER IN THE CLOSET, PUT THE WRAPPING PAPER ON THE TABLE, POUR DRUNK SHELLY A GLASS OF WINE...

SHELLY. Oh everybody's a comedian!

DONNIE. FIND THE SNOWMAN ON THE TREE AND... PLAY "HAVE YOURSELF A MERRY LITTLE CHRISTMAS" ON THE PIANO. Okay. I got it.

>   (**AVERIE** *has pulled out her phone and takes a*
>   *photo of* **DONNIE**.)

AVERIE. Donnie! Smile. *(She takes the selfie.)* You look crazy!

FIDEL. GO!

>   (**DONNIE** *begins the task of walking toward the*
>   *closet. Turns out to be the front door.* **ADAM** *jumps*
>   *in to help navigate him away from the front door.)*

ADAM. Front door.

DONNIE. The door looks the same.

>   *(He opens the closet door and begins his search for*
>   *the blue sweater.)*

What am I looking for?

ADAM. The –

JACKIE. Shh, you're not supposed to help.

ADAM. Right.

DONNIE. A blue sweater.

>   *(He struggles to find this.)*

This is black. A black coat. *(He tosses the coat on the floor.)*
I need a sweater. Blue. A blue sweater.

>   *(He finds his mother's blue cardigan.)*

I got the blue sweater.

SHELLY. I don't understand why this is the right time to
play games.

>   *(He holds the sweater and then thinks of the next*
>   *task.)*

DONNIE. Now I was supposed to do what now? Snowman.
A snowman on the tree. I'll put this here. Do I need to
keep it? Or put it down or something.

>   *(No one answers. They begin to get wrapped up in*
>   *the exercise.)*

I'll put it down.

>   *(He looks around for the best place to put it down.*
>   *He crosses around the couch and slams into the*

endtable. Frustrated, he throws the sweater on the ground.)

Ow, shit.

DOTTY. Keep going Son.

DONNIE. Oh my God I can't hear myself think. What was I doing?

(He begins to get very annoyed and panicky.)

Snowman. Snowman. THIS NOISE IS DRIVING ME CRAZY! OK. OK. Alright. Alright. FUUUCK! My fucking feet are fucking killing me.

(He begins to head for the tree.)

Where did I just put the sweater? The blue sweater. I found the blue sweater. Now the snowman.

No the snowman would be on the tree.

*(Distracted by coats on the floor, **DONNIE** heads back to the closet instead and shoves the coats in.)*

Now what?

SHELLY. POUR ME A GLASS OF WINE.

AVERIE. Shhhh –

DONNIE. Right.

*(**DONNIE** stumbles around to the coffee table.)*

Wine. Wine. This isn't wine. Is this hot sauce?

AVERIE. Boy, gimme my hot sauce.

*(**DONNIE** exits into the dining room.)*

DONNIE. Wrong. I can't find it. Is there wine in here or in the living room? Is it on the table?

DOTTY. That's it Son, that's enough.

(He comes back into the living room.)

DONNIE. Did I get the snowman on the tree? I'll get that and then I will worry about your wine. I can't THINK!

(He goes over to the tree.)

JACKIE. Be careful! The TREE!

DONNIE. WHAT?

> (**DONNIE** *turns to hear* **JACKIE**, *tree in hand, and almost brings it down.*)

> (*Everyone panics. This stops* **DONNIE** *in his tracks. He tears off headphones and goggles.* **DOTTY** *goes to* **DONNIE**.)

DOTTY. You see.

> (*Silence.*)

> (*Silence.*)

> (*Silence.*)

> (*Silence.*)

> (*Silence.*)

> (**DONNIE** *rips off the tape, latex gloves and kicks off his shoes. He now understands the trauma, the reality of what his mother is going through, or what she will go through.*)

DONNIE. When is dinner time? I need to eat!

ADAM. Donnie are you okay?

SHELLY. I have to get Jason and then we'll eat.

AVERIE. HOLD UP! Donnie. You alright?

> (**DONNIE**, *unhinged, goes off to the dining room.*)

ADAM. Donnie you alright?

AVERIE. You sweating.

DOTTY. You understand. He understands.

FIDEL. It's the virtual dementia experience, we found it online.

ADAM. Maybe you should have gotten the actual kit, I think there is an actual kit.

> (**ADAM** *and* **SHELLY** *go after* **DONNIE**.)

SHELLY. IT'S NOT TIME YET!

DONNIE. IT'S TIME! THE BELL HAS GONE OFF! I'M AWAKE.

AVERIE. What the fuck?

ADAM. DONNIE CALM DOWN. YOU'RE HAVING ANOTHER ANXIETY ATTACK!

SHELLY. Donnie put that down –

AVERIE. Stop controlling people.

DOTTY. You understand.

> (**DOTTY** *turns on the recorder. She is very still with a serene smile on her face, taking in this pandemonium.*)

FIDEL. Your feet are in her shoes.

SHELLY. Donnie you are ruining dinner!

DONNIE. I shouldn't have come home!

> (**DONNIE** *enters, followed by* **ADAM** *and* **SHELLY**.*)

DOTTY. JASON!

SHELLY. Jason is not here Mom.

ADAM. Everything is fine.

DONNIE. Everything is not fine.

ADAM. So let's do the work.

DONNIE. We have to get her what she needs.

SHELLY. Finally things are starting to make sense around here.

AVERIE. You alright Mom? Why is the tape recorder on? Mom?

> (*She doesn't acknowledge her daughter.*)

DONNIE. Everything is in danger of vanishing. You, me, all of us.

ADAM. It is! And that's LIFE!

AVERIE. Mom?

SHELLY. Mom I'm taking you upstairs.

DONNIE. Stop bossing us around!

AVERIE. Yeah, you ain't the boss of me!

SHELLY. *(She flips her wig.)* I'M JUST TRYING TO GET SOME SANITY IN THIS HOUSE!

JACKIE. I should go.

AVERIE. Bye, girl, bye!

ADAM. Donnie, stop it with the food.

DONNIE. Why, because I am so fucking old and obese?

ADAM. I NEVER SAID THAT!

DONNIE. YOU DID.

ADAM. NO, I DIDN'T!

AVERIE. Who gives a shit! There is a woman with ALZHEIMER'S IN THIS HOUSE you selfish fucks.

> *(The sound of a text message on* **AVERIE**'s *phone comes in. She checks her phone.)*

DONNIE. When I was thirteen, I thought I would be my best at forty! Didn't we Jackie?

JACKIE. Ummmm? –

DONNIE. We looked forward to forty! Knowing more. Right?

JACKIE. I'm a mess.

DONNIE. I want to grow gray hair and wear AGE APPROPRIATE clothes. No! I don't want to do Tina, or Molly, or some other drug that sounds like your best white girlfriend!

JACKIE. *(Whimpers.)* I USED TO BE YOUR BEST WHITE GIRLFRIEND!

> *(***JACKIE*** *bursts into a flood of tears and runs into the kitchen.)*

DONNIE. I WANT TO BE A DADDY!

ADAM. Is this what is going on with you? A midlife crisis?

AVERIE. You alright Mom? She's not answering me y'all? Mom you alright?

SHELLY. *(Soberly.)* Take her upstairs!

DONNIE. I don't want to put her to sleep!

SHELLY. I don't want to put her to sleep either. She's fading away, can't you see!

DONNIE. You can't control everything Shelly!

ADAM. I'll get the Xanax!

(**ADAM** *charges upstairs.*)

SHELLY. I know I can't control everything. It's happening.

(**DOTTY** *just smiles and stares off into space.*)

(*Silence.*)

I've watched it everyday.

AVERIE. (*Whispered.*) Mom?

SHELLY. This doesn't get better.

AVERIE. (*Whispered.*) Mom?

SHELLY. In and out, In and out, In and out. Till one day it's just out.

AVERIE. (*Whispered.*) Mom do you hear me?

(*Silence.*)

(*Silence.*)

(*Silence.*)

(**AVERIE** *grabs a hairbrush and begins brushing her mother's hair lovingly.*)

(**DONNIE** *goes over to the piano and bangs on the keys.*)

DOTTY. Play it Son. Play it for Grandma.

(**DONNIE**'s *banging turns into "HAVE YOURSELF A MERRY LITTLE CHRISTMAS."**)

(**AVERIE** *calmly continues to brush her mother's hair.*)

Grandma always wore white for some reason. Her hair in big Indian braids.

AVERIE. Mom? Why are you talking about Grandma.

DOTTY. What?

AVERIE. Mom?

(*Silence.*)

---

* A license to produce *Dot* does not include a performance license for "Have Yourself a Merry Little Christmas." Please see Music Use Note on page 3 for further information.

Mom?

DOTTY. Yes?

AVERIE. Do you know who I am?

DOTTY. Why you asking me that? Of course I do. Yes, you're my baby.

AVERIE. Yes, I'm your baby, Mommy.

> (**SHELLY** *begins to clean up.*)

DOTTY. (*Referring to* **SHELLY**.) Who's that cleaning lady? I don't know her.

> (*This hits* **SHELLY** *like a ton of bricks.*)

AVERIE. That's Shelly Mom.

DOTTY. Shelly?

AVERIE. And that's Donnie.

DOTTY. (*To* **DONNIE**.) Looking just like your father. Descendants of the Masai.

> (**DONNIE** *plays tenderly.*)

AVERIE. Come on Mom, let me take you upstairs.

DOTTY. Who put the stairs over here? Did we move?

AVERIE. No Mom. We're still here.

> (**AVERIE** *and* **DOTTY** *start to go upstairs.* **DOTTY** *looks over to* **DONNIE** *playing.*)

DOTTY. (*Lovingly calling out.*) Richard.

> (**AVERIE** *and* **DOTTY** *exit.*)
>
> (**DONNIE** *continues to play.*)

SHELLY. (*She begins to crack.*) I'm the cleaning lady. I'm the cleaning lady.

> (**SHELLY** *goes down into the basement.*)

WRAPPING IT ALL FOR JASON

(**DONNIE** *continues to play the piano in the living room. The scene transitions to late that night. Everything is cleaned up. Blue Spruce glitters in all its glory.* **ADAM** *comes down the stairs and just watches* **DONNIE** *playing.*)

ADAM. *(Lovingly.)* It's four a.m., you ever coming up?

(**DONNIE** *doesn't look at* **ADAM**. *He just plays.* **ADAM** *waits for a bit, then –.*)

DONNIE. It's something, the way your hands remember something that you thought was lost long ago. Locked deep in your memory. I haven't played in years. I didn't know that I could anymore.

(He plays the piano with his back to **ADAM**.*)*

My dad made sure that I had lessons. He told me that his father told him not to do any hard labor but either heal or do beautiful things with his hands.

ADAM. You told me how much of a respected doctor he was.

DONNIE. I lied. (**DONNIE** *stops playing.*) He wasn't. He was a broken man. His drinking got in the way of his practice. I played the piano for him.

ADAM. How come you never told me you played piano?

DONNIE. I do. I haven't played in years.

ADAM. Not bad.

DONNIE. We would have these family gatherings where we were our own little musical evening. Shelly doing some dance from *Swan Lake*, Averie singing her heart out and me on piano. At the best of times we appeared to be the perfect little middle class family. Then…when Dad died…suddenly, that just sent us all reeling. Trying to patch up the hole that he left in this family a long time ago. He was a sad man. I only really played for him. (**DONNIE** *plays again.*) We were his dreams for this neighborhood.

ADAM. I think you all made good on his dreams.

>(**ADAM** *crosses to record player.*)

>(**ADAM** *puts a soft and chill Christmas instrumental on the record player.** **DONNIE** *still keeps his focus off of* **ADAM**.)

ADAM. I made you a mixtape for Christmas. It's under the tree.

DONNIE. *(Bitterly.)* That is so retro. Dope.

ADAM. Sometimes I forget. We all forget that we are carrying baggage. And when we least expect it, our baggage will sneak up and punch us in the throat.

DONNIE. Punch us in the throat?

ADAM. OK, well not, punch us in the throat...rear its ugly little head. And that's okay. It's okay. I think being family, we have to know that and try to be patient with one another. Because love is there. I sound stupid.

DONNIE. No, you sound alright.

ADAM. I don't care about anything more than YOU. We may get lost sometimes, but I hope we can always find our way back to each other.

DONNIE. Is that line from a movie?

ADAM. *Sex and the City 2.*

>(*They share a bittersweet laugh.* **DONNIE** *still keeps his eyes off of* **ADAM**.)

DONNIE. I don't want to be like that guy...that guy who wrote that book. *The Right Side of 40? The Complete Guide to Happiness for Gay Men at Midlife and Beyond?*

ADAM. I didn't read it.

DONNIE. He was all about forty being the new thirty. He killed himself at forty-eight and there was a note that

---

*A license to produce *Dot* does not include a performance license for use of any copyrighted music. Samuel French and the author suggest that licensees use a song in the public domain or create an original composition.

he left that said, "It's a lie based on bad information," with an arrow pointing toward the title of the book!

ADAM. Wow.

DONNIE. Yeah, wow.

ADAM. I don't know – maybe I am having a little bit of a midlife crisis, but honestly I think it just takes some gays longer to finally express themselves, and POSSIBLY we do revert to these high school archetypes because, let's face it high school was TERRIBLE for us. I was a nerd. And so were you! And now at forty and we can afford to have the things that we missed out on we are just trying it on for size. But that stuff doesn't last. I know this! I want a family. I want what you want. And I don't care if you've got a little around the middle! I just want us to be healthy. *(Suddenly deeply emotional.)* Because I want you and I to be around for a long time.

> *(DONNIE finally gives in and looks at ADAM.)*

You're my best friend. Be patient with me. I love you chipmunk.

> *(ADAM kisses DONNIE sweetly. JACKIE walks in, sees this and walks straight back out.)*

DONNIE. And I did look good in those skinny jeans!

ADAM. I have the same pair – get another color!

JACKIE. *(Loudly, as she enters.)* I don't know how long I can lay on the floor of your kitchen. I should go home. It's late.

DONNIE. I'm sorry for the little floor show tonight.

JACKIE. Don't be sorry. Are you okay?

DONNIE. I think so. I'm okay.

JACKIE. It's the holidays. *(Beat.)* Everyone is just okay. It was good to see you Donnie. Adam.

ADAM. We should walk you home.

JACKIE. Oh no, I'm fine.

DONNIE. No, you can't walk out there at this time of night by yourself.

JACKIE. It's actually almost time for the sun to come up. It's quiet. I like this time of night or...day.

DONNIE. James Baldwin says that four a.m. is the most devastating hour.

JACKIE. Why?

DONNIE. Because you have a choice to stay in the darkness or prepare for the light. Because there will always be light.

JACKIE. *(Deeply emotional.)* I like that. There will always be light. I will hold on to that.

ADAM. That contemporary black writers course we took together really paid off.

DONNIE. Did you know that Bell Hooks is doing a "Ted Talk" next month?

ADAM. Oh, we got to go!

DONNIE. We gotta go.

JACKIE. Bell Hooks is a fierce woman. Fierce.

DONNIE. You are just as fierce. You are going to be alright. Shelly told me that you are pregnant.

JACKIE. Damn. I told Shelly not to tell you.

DONNIE. Then why'd you tell her?

JACKIE. You got a point. I don't know. I needed some perspective, I guess. On this messy thing called life.

DONNIE. It's messy as fuck.

JACKIE. And I am WINNING!

DONNIE. You'll be alright.

JACKIE. You know, you fucked me up for any other man.

DONNIE. Don't be silly, we were kids.

JACKIE. You were my first. And you were so nice. And sweet. And funny.

DONNIE. And gay.

JACKIE. Gay boys make the best husbands. They do you know?

ADAM. They do.

DONNIE. You are so crazy Jackie.

JACKIE. When did you know? I mean, did you know even when you were with me?

DONNIE. We are not having this conversation. We were together over twenty years ago.

JACKIE. I never got a chance to ask.

(*Silence. They both look at* **ADAM**. **ADAM** *looks away to give them their moment.*)

DONNIE. Well… I fought it, you know? I had no role models of what being gay was. So… I was with my closest friend. The funny and pretty girl from around the corner that I laughed the most with.

(*Silence.*)

JACKIE. So… I didn't turn you gay?

DONNIE. You can't turn somebody gay, stupid.

JACKIE. Aww you called me stupid. Like old times.

(**JACKIE** *kisses* **DONNIE** *on the lips. Silence.* **ADAM** *sees this.*)

Nothing? Really. Nothing?

(*They laugh.*)

But you look so STRAIGHT! You look good!

DONNIE. That's how the gay boys do it. Gotta stay healthy and fit! I want to be around for a long time.
I got a lot to stay around for.

JACKIE. Well… I got a late Zipcar. They are going to be in my ass.

DONNIE. You drove a Zipcar down here?

JACKIE. I was on the lam.

ADAM. From who or where? (**ADAM** *helps* **JACKIE** *into her coat.*)

JACKIE. From New York. From A Hot Latin Married Man. Me. My choices. Probably stemmed from the loss of my parents, having a gay high school sweetheart, and being a white girl who grew up in an all black neighborhood. You process a lot on a kitchen floor late at night.

DONNIE. Or having a full on meltdown in front of your family on Christmas Eve.

JACKIE. That was full out.

DONNIE. I just got off of a fast.

JACKIE. A detox will fuck you up.

DONNIE. Trying to make healthy choices will do that.

(**DONNIE** *puts his coat and shoes on.*)

ADAM. We know you feel safe, but we are gonna walk you home.

JACKIE. Okay. Okay. It's the hood, THE HOOD! *(Beat.)* I heard you two making up. I am glad you can do that. Nice to see when a couple can work it out. I'm telling you. It's dark out here! You have to fight for one another. Not that I know, I'm chronically single! But from what I see out here, that is the best kind of love. The love when you fight to love each other. Fight to hold on.

(**SHELLY** *comes up from the basement with a trunk.*)

SHELLY. She has been fighting to hold on for a while.

ADAM. What are you doing up, it's almost dawn.

SHELLY. I'm up.

DONNIE. She's up.

SHELLY. Looking through this old trunk filled with family albums, report cards, newspaper clippings of when Clinton won –

JACKIE. Obama won –

DONNIE. Family reunion t-shirts –

SHELLY. Cassette tapes... Trying to hold the memories. Locking them in a box. Fighting to hold on. OH MY GOD! WHAT TIME IS IT?! I FORGOT TO PICK UP MY SON!

(**AVERIE** *has come down the stairs.*)

AVERIE. I went and picked Jason up from your neighbors after I put Mom to bed. He is sleeping in my old room.

I thought you needed some time to yourself down there. I mean, you got me and Jason at home, Mom over here, you work all the time. You're welcome.

SHELLY. Well...thank you. Is Mom alright?

(Silence.)

AVERIE. No she's not. She won't ever be alright again. That is our new normal. We need to sit down and talk rationally, and see what needs to happen.

SHELLY. That's what I've been –

AVERIE. No, rationally. Around a table, at a decent hour, and most importantly we have to involve her. We can't talk AROUND her, Shelly. She needs to be there, in the conversation, whether she is fully present or not.

DONNIE. She's right.

SHELLY. She is. Oh my God. You're RIGHT.

AVERIE. Not always.

SHELLY. I'm a pain in the ass. //

AVERIE. You mean well. //

DONNIE. Language. //

SHELLY. And so are you.

DONNIE. Me?

AVERIE. Yes, you're a pain in the ass.

DONNIE. I know.

SHELLY. Especially to him.

ADAM. I'm a pain in the ass too.

AVERIE. You're perfect for each other.

ADAM. We're working on it.

JACKIE. *(Outburst.)* FIGHT TO LOVE EACH OTHER! Fuck. I'm sorry, my fucking hormones. I'm starving.

ADAM. Me too. I heard there was some chicken in the fridge. You want some?

JACKIE. Oh my God, is it fried?

DONNIE. It is fried in buttermilk and the crust is crunchy –

*(**ADAM** and **JACKIE** run into the kitchen.)*

(Silence.)

AVERIE. White people LOVE fried chicken. *(Beat.)* Shelly, I'm going to move in here for a while if it's okay with Mom –

SHELLY. Um… Okay –

AVERIE. Get out of your basement and help out more, like I should –

SHELLY. Okay –

AVERIE. That's what I can do right now. Until I can make some REAL money –

SHELLY. Fine.

AVERIE. I know.

SHELLY. Fine.

AVERIE. I'mma take you and Mommy out for a girls' day. Get our hair whipped and some mani/pedi lovin.' My treat.

SHELLY. That will be nice. 'Cause I ain't going to Andre no more!

AVERIE. Your hair looks terrible!

SHELLY. I know.

AVERIE. Your hair does look terrible!

*(**FIDEL** comes down the stairs.)*

SHELLY. Fidel what are you still doing here? You should have gone home.

FIDEL. It's okay. It's good to be here. I don't mind.

SHELLY. Don't you have your own family you should be spending Christmas with?

FIDEL. In Kazakhstan.

SHELLY. Oh okay.

AVERIE. THAT'S how you pronounce it!

DONNIE. When's the last time you've been home?

FIDEL. Nine years ago.

DONNIE. Nine years ago!

AVERIE. Did he say nine years ago?

SHELLY. Is there an echo? He said nine years ago.

AVERIE. Why?

FIDEL. Well… I have been trying to get my asylum. Political asylum. You can be hurt if you are political activist in my country.

SHELLY. You are a political activist? In what way?

AVERIE. Yeah in what way? Something we should be worried about?

FIDEL. Oh, no, no, no. I just fight for human rights. Speak out for poor people, government corruption, things like that.

AVERIE. Alright, Al Sharpton.

FIDEL. But that is a no-no.

SHELLY. That can cost you your life where you're from.

FIDEL. I know. I left and came to this country. It was an opportunity for a better life. I taught myself English by watching the movies *My Best Friend's Wedding* and *Poetic Justice*. You know those?

AVERIE. Regina King is the truth.

FIDEL. I watched them over and over again. And lots of TV. You learn so much more than English. You learn behavior. Um, how can I say this? African American people are just like Kazakh's. Just another color. You are very colorful.

AVERIE. Colorful?

FIDEL. Especially you. Remind me of my sister. Everyone has a sister like you at home.

AVERIE. I even blew up in Kazakhstan! Woop Woop!

FIDEL. I haven't been able to figure out how it all works here, and it is hard, but I try. It's better than home. Although I miss my home.

SHELLY. Don't you have an immigration attorney?

FIDEL. I hope so. Mrs. Shealy put a copy of my case in a folder for you.

SHELLY. Is that what that was?

AVERIE. Help him Shelly.

SHELLY. I am a public defender.

AVERIE. You can help him, Shelly.

SHELLY. I don't know anything about immigration.

AVERIE. You can figure it out. We depend on you for that. In spite of myself, it's true. You're no Iyanla, but you do try to fix my life.

SHELLY. What I need to do is share some of the responsibility. Right?

AVERIE. You're right.

DONNIE. Right.

AVERIE. Bad habit, putting it on you. Just comes natural.

SHELLY. And I'm so bossy, it actually makes sense.

AVERIE. Fidel, we gon' try to help you work this out, Boo Boo.

FIDEL. You go, GIRL!

AVERIE. You go, BOY!

> (**FIDEL**'s alarm goes off! It is that same horrible alarm! Everyone reacts with an expletive of their choice.)

SHELLY. That alarm is HORRIBLE –

AVERIE. BOY I ALMOST LIT YOU UP!

DONNIE. I ALREADY HAD ONE FIT!

> (**DOTTY** enters from upstairs. She is in a haze.)

FIDEL. I'M SORRY! I'M SORRY, BUT IT'S TIME!

DOTTY. (She speaks as if she is in a haze) It's time.

FIDEL. IT'S TIME!

SHELLY. You okay Mom?

> (She is not. She is in a state that we have not seen. She is fragile and is in a bit of a fog.)

DOTTY. I wanna see the look on his face. It's time!

> (Silence.)
>
> (Silence.)
>
> (Silence.)

(AVERIE, SHELLY, and DONNIE look at each other. Helpless and not knowing exactly what to do. AVERIE assumes a new role. Leader. Hearts are broken but they are forging ahead.)

AVERIE. ALRIGHT! WE ABOUT TO HAVE A MERRY MERRY GATDAMNED CHRISTMAS! Ahem! I'd like to sing a little carol if you all don't mind. I am in GOOD VOICE! I got a text from my agent last night in the middle of Donnie's fit, that I got an audition for *America's Singing They Ass Off* or something like that! I'm about to blow up! Kaboom! Donnie will you tinkle the ivories?

DONNIE. I'll tinkle.

AVERIE. Not BANG the ivories!

DONNIE. I'll tinkle.

(DONNIE gets on the piano and plays. AVERIE sings "HAVE YOURSELF A MERRY LITTLE CHRISTMAS" in a very jazzy way.*)

SHELLY. *(Whispers.)* Mom? Your tape recorder.

DOTTY. What do you want me to do with that?

SHELLY. Didn't you want to record this?

DOTTY. What time is it?

(SHELLY turns on the tape recorder.)

SHELLY. You are recording this for Jason.

DOTTY. The little boy that delivers newspapers? I owe him for last week. Where's my purse?

(DOTTY goes to the dining and gets her purse. She pulls out a five-dollar bill and goes to the door. She opens it. In anticipation, she stands facing the open door.)

---

*A license to produce *Dot* does not include a performance license for "Have Yourself a Merry Little Christmas." Please see Music Use Note on page 3 for further information.

SHELLY. *(Into tape recorder.)* Son. This is the moment before you come down on Christmas Day. Our last Christmas all together as the family that you know.

> *(**SHELLY** emotionally cracks and **AVERIE** stops singing and goes to her.)*

AVERIE. But that's alright! This is your auntie. The sexy one. It's alright because things never stay the same, and we gotta roll with the punches. Make some sh-, damn, sorry.

SHELLY. MAKE SOME SHIT OUT OF IT!

> *(**FIDEL** goes over to **DOTTY**. Does his **DOTTY** routine of "Buy a girl a drink.")*

FIDEL. Buy a girl a drink?

> *(**DOTTY** and **FIDEL** laugh.)*

SHELLY. What the hell?

FIDEL. It's Christmas!

SHELLY. It's Christmas! *(Whispers into the tape recorder.)* Remember this. Remember all of this. *(Calling **ADAM** and **JACKIE** from the kitchen.)* It's time. JASON IT'S TIME!

AVERIE & DONNIE. IT'S TIME! //

> *(Everyone is yelling up the stairs for Jason.)*

ALL. // Merry Christmas!

> *(**DOTTY** takes the box of memories downstage. The look on her face is uncertain. It is filled with laughter, tears, pain, heartbreak, rage, and sadness. Where do we go from here?)*
>
> *(Blackout.)*

End of Play

CPSIA information can be obtained
at www.ICGtesting.com
Printed in the USA
BVOW10s0724140417
481243BV00014B/197/P